GROWING WITH DANCE

Developing through Creative Dance from Ages Two to Six

Moira Morningstar

Windborne Publications

© 1986 Windborne Publications
All rights reserved. Published 1986
Printed in Canada
Third Printing 1990

Canadian Cataloguing in Publication Data
Morningstar, Moira.
   Growing with dance

   ISBN 0-921179-00-6
   1. Movement education.   2. Dancing - Study
and teaching (Preschool)   3. Child development.
I. Title.
GV452.M67 1986   793.3'0880543   C86-091168-3

Additional copies of this book may be obtained from
Windborne Publications, Order Dept.
(Canada) P.O. Box 359, Heriot Bay, B.C. V0P 1H0

To my children
Bronwen, Mark, and David

CONTENTS

Chapter Eight: **Stage Three—From about four and a half
to six years old inclusive**   131
(Mature four and a half year olds who have covered most of the
ground in Chapter Seven should be ready for this chapter. Beginning
five year olds should do most of the Chapter Seven activities before
tackling the content of Chapter Eight. In any case some repetition
from Chapter Seven will be beneficial.)

LIST OF STORIES AND POEMS

PREFACE

A child is a discoverer. He is an amorphous, splen-
did being in search of his own proper form.

—Maria Montessori

How do we teach creative dance to children between two and six years old? How can we involve them deeply and joyfully at their own levels of development, and what material can we use?

This book attempts to answer these questions. It has been written in response to an ever-growing number of requests on how, why, when, and what to teach. It gives many examples of how to reach and teach small children in their own space according to maturity, temperament, and immediate need. It is geared to their changing growth patterns, offering suitable stimuli for development. Detailed resource material is also given including stories, poems, movement games, and music suggestions.

Content is based on the trial and error of experience, and only the material which has consistently worked is included. Theory, where given, has followed practice, and is based on a ten year study of teaching and observing well over a thousand children from varied backgrounds. Quotes from educators and others have been given in order to substantiate the philosophy formed in the process of working with the children.

Teaching creative dance to preschoolers is a challenging delight for which a sense of play and response to the unique moment are preferable to an academic approach. It is hoped, therefore, that while this book may provide a practical and theoretical basis for teaching, it also may inspire the spirit of innovation and further discovery.

ACKNOWLEDGEMENTS

Special thanks to the two photographers: Liz Grambert (University of Victoria, Audio Visual and Television Services) for her delightful portrait-like full page photographs; and E. Lyn Lewis for capturing the action of the younger children so well in the half page photographs.

Many thanks to the students of Camosun College (Early Childhood Education and Care program) for their fine contributions to Outdoor Movement, Chapter Nine.

A most appreciative thank you to Steve Spyker for helping me with my final editing and proofreading.

I want to thank the following three remarkable women for their example and inspiration:

• "Madame Fedro", who I understand was once the Prima Ballerina of the Ballet Joos, and who taught me Movement at the Preparatory Academy to the Royal Academy of Dramatic Art, in London, many years ago. She conveyed the magic of movement so dynamically that my inability to reproduce it at that time filled me with such frustration that it became a spur to effort and discovery!

• Marian Thomas, who trained under Maria Montessori herself, and who taught my own three children at her Montessori School in Metchosin, British Columbia. She profoundly impressed me in that through keen observation she never ceased to learn from the children under her care. She taught with love, creating a beautiful and wholesome atmosphere. She respected the unique and wonderful being of each child.

• Joyce Boorman who is not only a fine educator and writer, but a most gifted teacher. Sixteen years ago I attended two workshop lectures given by her at the Banff School of Fine Arts. They were on Creative Dance in the first three grades, and were most inspiring. Afterwards I went up to her and said that I too would like to teach Creative Dance, but that I lacked experience in this field. She looked me straight in the eye and said, "Do it! A lot of people will be glad that you did."

CHAPTER ONE

CREATIVE DANCE

But only the dance is sure!
make it your own.
Who can tell
what is to come of it?

—William Carlos Williams

What creative dance is

A creative dance is one in which you create and communicate your own movements; it has form, variety, and expressiveness. You often work around a theme, and as your dance evolves you may wish to repeat and modify it giving it a beginning, a middle, and an end, perfecting it as you go. A creative dance may be a group project.

Haphazard movement is not creative dance. When very small children discover different ways of moving and when they jump, bob, and jiggle repetitively to music, they are not really doing creative dance, but they are learning a vocabulary of movement out of which creative dance may later evolve.

It is very difficult to say where discovery and repetition of movement end and where creative dance begins, but it depends on the ability to hold onto a nucleus of thought and to create a pattern. It also requires a growing artistic sense of movement. Creative dance often begins to emerge from the foundation of experimental movement around five years old.

Dance is the poetry of movement, and one cannot just "do"

creative dance without having gone through the preceding stages of movement discovery. To make a parallel with art, the child who eventually draws a tree must first make scribbles and random lines. The tiny child who is scribbling, however, is deriving just as much benefit from practicing art as the older one who creates pictures. The same idea holds true for dancing. Learning and development take place through whatever stage of rhythmic movement the child is capable of as he gradually progresses into creative dance.

What creative dance does for the individual

Creative dance promotes coordination of thought, feeling, and action because it is developed from the inside of the child outwards instead of being imposed from the outside in! Whereas most educational processes divide the mind-body connection by dealing with a human being in separate parts (physical education for the body, academic subjects for the brain, etc.) creative dance integrates the mind-body connection by dealing with the human being as a unit.

As space and time are explored by the child through movement, so the image of the body develops in the brain. As the body image develops so does the concept of the physical environment. In the words of Maria Montessori, "Movement is not only an expression of the ego but it is an indispensable factor in the development of consciousness, since it is the only real means which places the ego in a clearly defined relationship with external reality." Furthermore, the developing sense of movement provides a mode of operation for the mind, just as the developing sense of speech does. For example, when we imagine any event which takes place in space and time, we are using our kinesthetic sense, or movement sense. (Our kinesthetic sense operates through the nerve ends in the muscles, tendons, and joints, which convey to our brain the sensations of movement and stillness, tension and relaxation.) An engineer, a choreographer, and a child learning to cross the road, all employ their kinesthetic sense when they project moving images in their minds. The finer this sense is developed, the greater is their level of success.

The creative dancing process not only helps to develop a clear body image and an acute kinesthetic sense, but it also helps to develop musicality and a sense of rhythm, imagination and creativity, the arts of listening and observing, and the skills of communicating and cooperating!

To sum up, learning creative dance has a wholistic educational value reaching far beyond that of specific movement training, and affecting the deep development of the human being.

What creative dance does for our society

Everyone can dance! All primitive societies dance and sing quite naturally. The dance has a high order of priority in the tribe and usually has a ritual as well as a festive significance. There is a North American Indian song from the Makah tribe which says:

Mine is a proud village, such as it is,

We are at our best when dancing.

At the moment dancing has a less revered position in our western society, and we take movement too much for granted. When children have discovered most of the actions necessary for getting around, we usually let movement take care of itself until the physical education stage at school. We fail to recognize that movement is one of the great learning tools of the young child, and overlook its creative possibilities. We forget that we are visceral as well as cerebral beings and that movement is a language, a means of understanding and communication.

Even ethnic dancing is rarely a part of the natural scene, but has become a subject to be "learnt". Whereas in a more simple society everybody dances and makes music, today we generally think that a dancer is one who has completed a specialized training. When we make a deliberate decision to go dancing or to attend a dancing class, most of us are self-conscious to some degree, and even those who have formal training are often made nervous by the thought of improvising. Thus, our society has lost a natural piece of itself, which leads to inhibition of spontaneous and expressive movement.

In offering creative dance to the children of our society we are trying once more to celebrate life through the dance, and to recover a sense of ease with movement. We are counterbalancing an urban culture which, in divorcing its roots from nature, also divides the mind from the body. We are building a more wholesome society.

CHAPTER TWO

METHODS

To structure or not to structure

There are those who believe that the best way of getting pre-schoolers to dance is to put on the music and let them get on with it. At the other end of the scale there are those who believe that pre-schoolers should be given a very specific learning structure to follow.

The unstructured approach, while providing a useful movement opportunity, is ultimately limited in scope. In reality some children don't "get on with it" when the music is put on, and those who *do* are often restricted by their immediate knowledge and disposition. For example, some children habitually move very fast without much control; others favor certain parts of the body when moving, to the exclusion of others; still others don't "hear" the mood and tempo of the music, so fail to relate to it.

The very structured approach is equally limiting, When denied the opportunity to discover for themselves, children are apt to become bored or processed and their dancing takes on a more mechanical aspect.

Note: Some of the content of this chapter may be obvious to those who continually work with small children. However, as it is anticipated that some of the readers are new to teaching either this age group or this subject, it is written without the assumption of prior knowledge.

A flexible teaching structure is the best suited for developing the child's full dancing potential as it allows, within bounds, for diversity of response. For example, the idea of stretching out and curling up could be explored as a group with the help of images and examples, and then the creation of new movement variations could be encouraged through suggestion. It must be remembered, however, that although the above scheme is appropriate for five year olds who very much like to innovate, a modified approach is needed for two and a half year olds who usually prefer to imitate. This is dealt with later in detail.

It would initially be easier for the teacher to opt for either a highly structured or a nonstructured method of teaching preschool creative dance. But the flexible structure, which must maintain a dynamic balance between these two approaches and be subject, like the walker on the tightrope, to constant readjustment, yields the best and most satisfying results. This is because it takes into account two of the most powerful inherent needs of children—the need to be secure in the known, and the need to reach forwards into the unknown.

How to teach creative dance in relationship to the small child's world

> *Childhood has ways of seeing, thinking and feeling peculiar to itself; nothing can be more foolish than to substitute our ways for them.*
> —*Jean Jacques Rousseau*

Very few books have been written on dancing for children below the age of four or five. A special approach is needed for the very young who are, on the whole, like little chameleons absorbing from their environment (in contrast to mature people who select from it). Having taught creative dance to all ages (including adult), the author is convinced of the need of a mode of presentation suitable to the developmental stage of the class.

Most adults take their own mode of perception for granted and are apt to forget the perspectives of very small children. But in order to understand the world of the very young, the adult mode of perception must be temporarily discarded. In fact it is useful to make a contrast between the abilities of children in the primary grades and those of two or three year olds, in order to know where to begin.

Older children have mastered basic movements and can reflect on what they are doing. Compare this with children of two or three years old who are still learning everyday movements and who are so taken up with the action that they rarely step outside it to think about *what* they are doing. When children of this age are asked to show you what dance they were just doing, they will almost always fail to remember it. Their movement memory is undeveloped because they have, as yet, no clear body image through which it can work.

Older children can readily appreciate sensory contrasts. Contrasts such as high and low, fast and slow, light and heavy, big and small, cannot be perceived clearly at first by small children. The dimensions and laws of our physical world as revealed through space, time, and weight are again first encountered through the body, and through continual usage in movement are later evaluated by the brain.

A child of up to about three and a half years old, for example, feels quite existential about space. "Will I go down the plughole too?" wonders a two year old, seeing the bath water gurgling down, and having no concept of size of self in relation to the hole. An airplane receding into the distance may be seen as getting smaller and smaller by a three year old, instead of getting further and further away. Space is simply an area in which "me" is in the middle! The idea that space exists independently and can be used as a medium in which to create direction, shape, and pattern is a concept which can only develop slowly. In this context, Jean Piaget, in his essay on "The Mental Development of the Child," says: "As for normal children, they are practically unanimous in believing that the moon accompanies them on a walk, and their egocentricity impedes them from thinking what the moon would do in the presence of people strolling in opposite directions."

Older children have some ability to manage and direct themselves in a group. The sense of cooperating in a group is alien to children under three, and "I want" predominates. Gradually, through watching and through moving alongside others, children learn *from* each other and then learn how to dance *with* each other. This has just as much to do with social development as with dancing.

Older children can easily be taught through the medium of words. The limited vocabulary of two and three year olds inhibits this form of communication. The dance movement of a two year old springs from instinctive response to rhythm and is extended through imitation. Words begin to be useful when the transition from instinctive movement to conscious creative movement takes place. At this time words aid; in giving instruction, "Let's do a very light dance so we can't hear our feet on the floor"; in evoking images, "How does a tree move in the wind?"; and in giving the essence of action, "Spin; stretch; freeze." Thus, while speaking in only the most simple, clear words to the youngest children, a teacher should develop an awareness of the growing verbal ability of her class and use it to develop dance further.

Older children can draw on a range of images as a basis for movement. It should be remembered that children, like the rest of us, can only imagine things that are based on experience; the younger the child, the more simple and familiar must be the images used. For example, a two and a half year old may not remember snow, so unless it is actually snowing there is no point in doing a snowflake dance. A six year old will not only be able to remember snow but will even be able to help in making up a story about the life of a snowflake and then translate it into an expressive dance.

Older children can usually differentiate between "real" and "imaginary" worlds. The friends and monsters in the fantasies of preschoolers are translations of feelings, and because feelings are "real" the boundaries between the external world and the inner imaginary world are often confused. For many little children witches *do* hide in cupboards and monsters *are* under the bed. Care, discretion and humor are therefore needed in using powerful dramatic images.

Older children have a fair attention span. preschoolers on the other hand, although capable of great concentration, usually need to change their focus of attention more frequently. For this reason it seems best for children under six to pursue different movement concepts, or themes, within one class. For example, the theme of expressing differing gradations of weight from very light movements to very heavy ones, or the theme of pursuing different levels and directions in space, could occupy an older group for quite a long time. But with a very young group it is not worth sacrificing the principle of keeping alive the interest to that of thoroughly working out each theme. In any case preschoolers learn more by gradual absorption and much repetition than by logical development.

To summarize—the immediate world of the small child should be taken as the starting point for teaching. As this world grows, so can the range and depth of what is being taught. Conversely, the creative dance experience extends the small child's universe through developing comprehension, awareness, and ability to function. In this way learning and development both complement and stimulate one another.

How to involve parents and others in charge

The adults who take care of preschoolers are usually intimately concerned in their activities. Children often reflect in a striking way the attitude of the adults who bring them, and therefore it is desirable to create an atmosphere of harmony and understanding regarding participation.

The private dance teacher will either need to keep in close contact with parents (in the case of those children attending from private homes) or with a teacher or supervisor (in the case of a group of children attending from some institution). The preschool teacher or supervisor who is teaching her own group of children, will again need to keep in contact with parents.

Communication can be promoted by spending time talking to the adult contacts whenever appropriate and possible; by handing out information sheets; and by holding "open house" from time to time at which adults can view a class in progress. The adults are usually most cooperative and receptive when kept informed. Not only may they give valuable background information on individual children, but they often choose to spend extra time dancing with them.

As parental responses strongly color children's reactions to dancing, ways in which parents can both help and hinder are described from time to time, with suggestions for implementation of positive approaches.

How to encourage preschool participation

If small children don't want to dance, they will simply stop! Unless there is a good reason to stop, the following pointers are useful ways to keep them involved and happy.

1) Suggest rather than order a movement.
"Let's all jump!", "How would you dance to this sound?", "See if you can show me how a frog moves!" and "Let's make ourselves very small!"—works better than "Jump everybody!", "Move like this!", "Be a frog!", and "Curl up!"

2) Do the action along with them at first. When they are older and more experienced they will look to you less for support.

3) Ask movement questions as if you were seeking the answer together. If children feel you are waiting for them to be "right" or "wrong" they will be less apt to demonstrate the answers.

4) Give liberal encouragement
It is particularly important to give encouragement to those who are least confident.

5) Observe the general mood of the class and adjust your teaching plan accordingly.
Don't be afraid to switch to another activity if the one specially planned is just not working out. Take the cue from the children. (Always have a few extra items on the lesson plan.)

How to cope with nonjoiners

There are usually one or two children in every class who are more slow to join in at first. They may be overwhelmed by people and surroundings and need time to feel comfortable. They require a friendly sense of acceptance and the knowledge that nobody will mind if they prefer to watch until they feel ready to join in.

Urging them to participate usually fails whereas a gently offered hand at the right time may succeed. If they shrink back from advances it is best to leave them alone and, like Little Bo-Peep's sheep, they will almost certainly "come home" of their own accord in due course. Parents sometimes worry when their children hang back. In this case it is important to reassure these parents that it is quite normal for some children (particularly the more sensitive ones) to want to observe for a while. Parental pressures such as, "Now remember you promised me you'd dance today!", almost always backfire. Children do not dance for Mother but for themselves!

The "watchers" are usually eager to go dancing, but on arrival simply prefer to observe. This may go on from one to several weeks before they literally get off the ground, but when they do it is interesting to note that they are usually as far along as the others and have been learning through the watching experience. (Often a "watcher" will dance the entire lesson on arriving home!)

What is the most suitable clothing to dance in?

Garments should allow for complete freedom of movement. Stretch clothing, trousers, shorts, leotards with or without footless tights, are all good. It is best to dance in bare feet as shoes impede freedom of movement and socks and stocking feet are slippery. If mother insists on shoes, light, non-skid slippers are second best.

How to cope with attitudes towards boys and dancing

Lamentably, dancing is still often considered to be a feminine pursuit only. In these days of opposition to sexual discrimination, parents are still sometimes reluctant to put their sons into a dancing class. (This is more apt to occur in the "private" dancing group than in day-care centers and kindergartens.) These same children then quickly absorb the mistaken idea that "boys don't dance!" However, reflection on the history of dancing denies this. In primitive societies men do nearly all the dancing, and ethnic dance traditions reveal than men do at least half the dancing.

When family and peers are unprejudiced as to sex roles in dancing, and in particular when father is in favor and will join in with his son at home, boys will take to creative dance with enormous enthusiasm, producing energetic, sensitive, and imaginative results. But while there is still a bias, it is useful for parents and teachers to encourage boys who are friends or neighbors to dance in the same group. Sometimes the substitution of the word "movement" for the inflammatory word "dance" is enough to dispel prejudice!

CHAPTER THREE

SOURCES AND RESOURCES

Musical Accompaniment: ways of using music to accompany the class

It is possible to teach creative movement along the lines of mime or dramatic movement or explorative gymnastics, without a sense of musical dynamics, but *creative dance* requires a musical dimension.

Dancing and music are closely related, and dancing down the ages has relied on musical accompaniment. Modern dance may use music as a mood background only. In this case the dance movement rhythms may not be regular in character but more loosely expressed as are the freer rhythms of blank verse. However, if they become too haphazard and if they are not linked in some way to the music, the movement will not attain the aesthetic quality of dance. Should the dance not use music at all, it must be strongly sustained by its own internal rhythms as if the music were being heard inside the dancer's head. Thus, dance is still linked to music through rhythm.

Every activity in this book is intended to be done within a rhythmic framework. This is important not only because the dance requires that it should be so, but because rhythm is a wonderful catalyst for bringing together mind, body, and feeling. As Emile

---

N.B. "Music" in this context means rhythmical accompaniment of all types, with or without the addition of melody and harmony.

Jaques-Dalcroze says in his book *Rhythm Music and Education,* "The study of rhythm conduces to develop not only the instincts for time, symmetry, and balance, but also—thanks to the training of the nervous system involved—the sensibilities.... The study of rhythmic movement awakens the whole organism."

Some schools of thought maintain that the child has good access to these internal rhythms, to which he should be allowed to move freely without the imposition of too much accompaniment. It is the conclusion of the author that the so-called internal rhythms are based on rhythms which have been heard. It is extremely likely that in the earliest years, the memory of the mother's heart-beat provides the basis for rhythmic movement, as is explained more fully in the next chapter. Also (after following up case histories) it appears that those children who seem to have the best sense of rhythm up to the age of six, are often those who have sung songs with their parents, or have been encouraged to *listen* to music and, possibly, to *make* simple music. (Listening to music does not mean being bombarded by a constant radio background which tends to dull the listening response as is further explained in Chapter Six.) In the words of Shinichi Suzuki, from his book *Nurtured by Love,* "We don't have to look for specific innate abilities or talents. It is a superior environment that has the greatest effect in creating superior abilities." Thus, while it is sometimes excellent for children to move at their own *pace* without accompaniment, it is clear that their sense of *inner* rhythm is fostered through listening to *outer* rhythm.

Music is a fine movement stimulus just as words and pictures are, but unlike words and pictures, music occupies the same time interval as dance and thus is especially evocative. Two to three year olds cannot dance without it!

It is certainly helpful if the preschool creative dance teacher can have a piano accompanist, and that this accompanist is a good improviser. Although this requires the addition of a piano to the list of equipment needed, and adds to the cost of the program, the investment is well worth it. However, the luxury of an accompanist is often impossible in terms of facilities and budget. This need not be a deterrent to teaching the subject, for whether there is a pianist or not, percussion instruments, clapping, and voice accompaniment, should be used. Commercial records used judiciously can also be helpful.

PERCUSSION INSTRUMENTS

Type	Special uses apart from maintaining the basic beat
•Hand Drum	Heavy or strong movements.
•Tambourine	"Tap" for travelling or sudden movements, "shake" for vibratory movements.
•Triangle	Light or delicate movements.
•Finger Cymbals	Light or delicate movements.
•String of Hand Bells	Light flopping movements.
•Rhythm Sticks (to be struck, one against the other)	Sharp incisive movements.
•Gong or Cymbal (one powerful stroke or a series of short ones)	Continuous movements (such as expanding, whirling, or rolling)
•Maraca or Rattle	Shaking, jiggling or vibratory movements.

THE VOICE

The voice can be used to accompany dance by:
1) Making rhythmic sounds—Yum Pum Pum or G-Doing
2) Making rhythmic word patterns—Tic-Toc says the clock
3) Singing—giving the addition of melody

HANDS AND FEET

Hands and feet can be used for clapping, tapping, or stamping, etc., to produce the basic beat.

THE PIANO

The piano is particularly good for accompanying dance as it is essentially a percussion instrument with a wide range of dynamic possibilities. Also melody and harmony can contribute to mood in a way that is obviously not possible on more simple percussion instruments. As previously mentioned, a pianist who can improvise in different rhythms and moods as well as one who can merely play from printed music, is a considerable asset.

THE GUITAR

The guitar is another very appropriate instrument for accompanying dance, and guitarists usually like to improvise.

A WIND OR STRING INSTRUMENT could be used to accompany but it would not be such a "natural" choice as piano or guitar.

MIXED METHODS OF ACCOMPANIMENT

A mixture of the above methods provides variety and interest. Percussion and Piano can be effectively used together—the percussion underlining the rhythmic beat.

COMMERCIAL RECORDS

These can be an interesting sound source and prove a valuable adjunct to teaching, but for regular use for the very young are less useful than live accompaniment. One cannot modify a record to suit the needs of the moment. A record sets the pace rather than adapts to it.

Throughout this book it is assumed that appropriate accompaniment of one sort of another will be provided as necessary. Where special effects are required, specific suggestions are made.

The creative dance teacher should be able to give a clear, rhythmic lead, as a fuzzy, hesitant lead invites confusion and disorder. The following are necessary basic rhythm requirements:

1) Ability to indicate a required rhythm and tempo to accompanist (if there is one) by clapping or tapping two or three bars first.
2) Ability to clap, beat on percussion instrument, or vocalize a variety or rhythms, in order to accompany the class.
3) Ability to speed these rhythms up or to slow them down, and to produce them quickly or slowly, lightly or heavily.
4) Ability to accent a chosen beat. For example, "No I *won't*" and "*No* I won't," have the same rhythm with a different accent.

Even with no previous experience in this area, these are not difficult skills to acquire, and a musical friend or a music teacher should be able to impart them in a fairly short time.

It is interesting to note that while dance may be developed through the use of music, musicality is also developed through dance. Emile Jaques-Dalcroze *(Rhythm Music and Education)* says: "The most potent element in music, and the nearest related to life, is rhythmic movement. . . . all the nuances of time—of energy (in music) can be 'realized' by our bodies, and the acuteness of our musical feeling will depend on the acuteness of our bodily sensations."

Stories and Poems

Stories which are based on a pattern of theme and variation, with a very simple development, are the best kind to use. Two traditional stories which follow this pattern are The Gingerbread Man and The Three Bears. Traditional stories, however, often have unhappy endings and frequently lack enough movement content to turn them into satisfactory dance exercises. In fact most children's literature, whether ancient or modern, lacks this continuous movement aspect, and therefore it is hard to find stories and poems which will work.

All the stories and poems in this book have been written for children's dance by the author with a view to inciting variety of movement. It is hoped that teachers will be able to add to the examples given here by making up their own from time to time. One way of making up a story is to create a central character (with whom it should be possible for children to identify) who needs something or someone, and who moves through a series of events to a satisfactory conclusion. (This follows the theme and variation pattern.) Another good plot is for the central character to have an adventure escaping from a difficult situation.

Poems for movement don't necessarily need to tell a story but can be descriptive in essence. Children seem to relate well to poems about nature reflecting aspects of the seasons, the weather, and the out-of-doors generally with which they are familiar.

As children, we usually have a vivid sense of being part of the natural world. Often, on the journey towards maturity, we lose the keenness of contact through the fragmentation of our natures in a multiplicity of arid tasks and procedures. Many city dwellers forget their ancient earth roots and lead lives of alienation in which they feel threatened by natural forces. If, as educators, we strive to nourish the sense of contact with nature that is inherent in childhood, we may in part help to prevent this split. (When we review the dances of our ancestors we see that they were permeated with this sense of nature.) So nature images for dancing—which can readily be presented through a poem—are food for the psyche as well as being practical suggestions for a dance.

Refrains in poems and stories—whether they be actual words or nonsense sounds—can be translated into corresponding movement refrains, and are both popular and effective for developing rhythm.

Gender of the central character in a story or poem may raise a potential problem, if each child in a mixed class is to identify with him/her. Perhaps the problem is mainly a concern of adults and the small child doesn't really mind whether he/she is dancing a male or a female role as long as the story is interesting and there is lots of action. One pragmatic way of dealing with gender is to alternate the sex of the central character each time the story or poem is told.

Musical accompaniment for a story or poem can be approached in various ways. The usual method of story dancing is to tell a short section and then to move to it immediately. In view of this sectional approach it would be possible, though time consuming, to illustrate with recorded musical excerpts. Again, it is very helpful if one has an accompanist who can improvise musical sounds with which to illustrate the piece, however percussion can provide the necessary rhythmic accompaniment.

A note on suitability of stories and poems for age groups other than those suggested.

Generally speaking, stories and poems from the youngest age group can be used for the middle one, and those from the middle age group can be used for the oldest one—whether specially indicated or not within the context of the chapters in which they occur.

Movement Games

Whereas an older group, capable of abstraction, would first study a dance concept and then incorporate it in a movement task, small children learn primarily through *doing,* and a movement game with a simple objective provides a good medium for this process. This book contains a variety of many such games, (also composed by the author).

A note on further Sources

Please see the Appendix for:

1) A note on the work of Rudolf Laban.
2) Bibliography of books on Early Childhood Education and books on Dance, giving brief descriptions of the same.
3) Recommended appropriate selections of music which are easily found on commercial records.
4) Recommended piano pieces which are readily available.
5) Recommended song books and poetry books.

CHAPTER FOUR

EARLIEST RHYTHM AND
MOVEMENT DEVELOPMENT

*There is no use judging children's abilities from the
training they receive five or six years after birth.
Abilities are born and developed by the working of
the vital forces of the organism as it strives to adapt
to its environment right in the beginning.*
—Shinichi Suzuki

A brief survey of early rhythm and movement development
before the age of two is given below to facilitate understanding of
the approach to preschool dance teaching, which follows on or-
ganically.

Experiences in rhythm and movement begin before birth, movement within the uterus occurring without sense of weight within
the amniotic fluid. Frederic Leboyer in his book *Birth Without
Violence* has this to say: "The embryo becomes the fetus; the plant
becomes the animal. Movement comes to it, beginning at the trunk,
spreading outward to the extremities. The fetus stirs, takes pleasure
in its limbs. And in its freedom. Supported by waters all around it,
the fetus is weightless, light as a bird, agile and lively as a fish." And
then he continues, "By the time babies are actually born, their ears
have already been serving them for a long time. While they are still
in the womb, the noises of their mothers' bodies reach them; joints
cracking, intestinal rumblings. And giving the rhythm to it all is the
strong drumbeat of the mother's heart."

The mother's heart-beat, now speeding up, now slowing down,
surely imprints its rhythmic sound deep in the developing con-

sciousness of the fetus; and it has been proved beyond doubt that the newborn can derive calming and comfort from being close to it. *The heart-beat rhythm, Dum-di Dum-di Dum-di Dum, is the one to which very small children best respond when starting to dance* and lends itself to rocking, bouncing, galloping, and swinging movements.

Once the baby is born diverse rhythms and movements begin to impinge in the new "unwatery" world—the all powerful rhythm of breathing, the first jerkings and thrustings of arms and legs in a world of gravity, the sense of being handled, rocked and moved in various ways by others. Then, as a contrast, the tiny baby experiences the extraordinary sense of stillness which was not so possible in the watery repercussions of the womb. Outside that shock-absorbing world, movement and stillness must feel more like dual states of being.

Although an infant is totally open to sense perception, organization of sensations must be learned—random sense experiences must be coordinated gradually into a growing coherence of environment. Romain Rolland gives a wonderful poetic description of this stage of awareness in his Nobel Prize winning book *Jean-Christophe*: "The room is a country, a day is a lifetime. How is a creature to know himself in the midst of these vast spaces? The world is so large! A creature is lost in it. And the faces, the actions, the movement, the noise, which make round about him an unending turmoil! . . . He is weary; his eyes close; he goes to sleep. . . . These first days come buzzing up in his mind like a field of corn or a wood stirred by the wind, and cast in shadow by the great fleeting clouds. . . . The shadows pass; the sun penetrates the forest. Jean-Christophe begins to find his way through the labyrinth of the day."

The parent can help the tiny child towards orientation. A new baby needs to be held, caressed, and cuddled as much as he needs milk. Not only is his spirit nourished through physical contact, but his body awareness begins to develop through the touch of others. Holding onto his hands and feet and gently moving his limbs creates a sensation of pleasure. Lifting, and particularly lowering, causes fright at first—unless done with great care and sensitivity. But later, when the child learns to trust the one who is holding, these sensations can become pleasant experiences. Muscles are developed when the infant attempts to move, first in small, and then in larger movements. Rolling over, crawling in some manner, sitting up, pulling on furniture, and finally, walking, eventually take place.

A very small baby enjoys listening to musical sounds—a tinkling bell or wind chimes, a shaking rattle, a music box, or a gentle singing voice, will often cause him to smile and gurgle with delight. A baby will make many vocal experiments and surprise himself. Most of us have seen the look of delight and puzzlement on the face of an infant who has just made a new noise and is trying to repeat it. Then, in due course, he will try to make sounds through other objects—by shaking a rattle, pushing a chiming ball, squeaking a teddy bear, etc.

It is interesting to observe how a child will unconsciously utilize rhythm in repetitive movements such as bouncing, or shaking his head back and forth, and in repetitive sounds such as "Da da da da da da da." The parents may help to develop the sense of rhythm by gently rocking their child, or by lightly "dancing" him on the feet while supporting the body weight. At several months, a child who is bounced on one's knee many times and then lifted high in the air to a phrase such as, "bouncy, bouncy, bouncy, bouncy, bouncy, bouncy, *uuuuuuuup* we go!" will usually respond with laughter. This response to the "breaking" of a given rhythm and movement is quite a sophisticated development.

Parents will often do all these things for a child from a natural sense of playfulness without realizing the fact that they are giving their child initial movement and music training.

Between the ages of one and two much development takes place as the child continually experiments with movement. Using trial and error the child goes further afield and explores the world in different ways. The climbing instinct is strong, but it takes longer to learn how to get down than up. Getting into, onto, over, under, and around things occupies a great deal of time, energy, and concentration. Moving other objects about also extends the sense of movement and balance in the child's own body, whether it be rocking a doll, pushing a dump-truck, rolling a ball, squishing play dough, building blocks, or hammering pegs.

Children of this age enjoy listening to nursery rhymes and jingles, though words and tunes are not as important as rhythms, which have a more basic impact. (Consider primitive music which usually consists of a strong, repeated rhythm with minimal melody, often hypnotic in its repetitive effect.)

To sum up—It seems that movement and rhythm are two of the early keys to the universe. *They can continue to be so if from now on their importance is honored through education and environment.*

CHAPTER FIVE

AN OVERVIEW OF AGES AND STAGES
BETWEEN TWO AND SIX YEARS OLD

Usually a child is two and a half years old before being ready to join in a dancing class experience, but before this it is profitable if a child gets together with one or both parents to roll, run, clap, thump, and generally move around to music.

The advantages of dancing at home are that the surroundings are very familiar and that the session can be short and informal. Children around two years old usually have a strong sense of *being* rather than of *knowing*. If other children are dancing in the room with them, they are simply experienced as part of their being-sphere and so are noticed only peripherally.

The main aim in dancing with children about this age is to make the whole experience a joyful one. Two year olds need to move spontaneously and, although they usually choose to imitate, they are apt to be quite contrary if they feel coerced into doing so. It is best to let them move in any way they like and to let them stop when they wish. Usually a supportive, playful duet ensues, led by mother or father, in which the child copies for a while, then may suddenly sit down to look at something, or else run to be picked up and hugged or swung through the air—then the "dance" continues.

Children who move with their parents or elders in this way have a head start in movement, rhythm, coordination, and physical confidence. Those who have never had the opportunity are usually far less able to move expressively to music when they are later given the opportunity to do so with other children. Fortunately this can be remedied gradually.

A few months later, at about the age of two and a half, the child's horizons have extended to where he will enjoy imitating a teacher as well as a parent. (Imitation is the natural mode of learning at this stage, and this is more fully explained in the next chapter.) Sometimes however, an assertive two and a half year old will "buck" at cooperating with a parent in a dance, but will feel his emerging sense of autonomy is less threatened by a teacher who is once removed from mother or father.

Between two and a half years old and six, there is a continual flow of development, but for purposes of teaching creative dance, it is useful to think of development occurring in three main stages.

The first stage is roughly two and a half to three and a half, when a child will benefit greatly from attending a class with a parent; but as both parents work in many households, this may prove difficult to work out. In this case volunteer adult helpers at the dancing session can improve the adult to child ratio with very good results.

The next stage is from about three and a half to four and a half or five. Here most children are happy to attend without adult support (apart from the teacher and perhaps an additional helper). They are now learning to be more innovative and adventurous.

The third stage runs from about four and a half to six years old, inclusive. Building on what they have already absorbed, children seem to go through a kind of creative budding from which exciting group work can be developed and in which new movements evolve continually.

Although ages are given as approximate indicators of stages in this book, they are only to be regarded as guidelines. Children develop at different rates and often in spurts. Between these spurts they may seem to be marking time for a while, but in reality they are consolidating their progress and inwardly preparing for the next growth period. A late developer may be just as gifted as an early one in the end.

Boys, at first, are quite often less coordinated than girls, less emotionally mature in a group context, and less apt to "listen", although they can improve this capacity when encouraged to do so. But around four or five years old they seem better able to sustain a dance at a very high energy level, and are more apt to produce original visual effects (i.e., a "cartoon" sense is more apparent in their movements). The author is not certain whether these differences are inborn or acquired, but has observed them sufficiently frequently to find them worthy of note.

With regard to individual development, it is important to realize the role that myelination plays. Myelination is the progressive coating of peripheral nerves with a fatty substance called myelin. This process improves conductivity of nerve impulses, and good coordination and nimble movement depend on it. Myelination develops from shoulders to fingers, hips to toes, and may be completed as early as three or as late as five years old. A child who is late "getting it together" may be just physically less mature than one who moves well, and such a child is not necessarily reflecting a slower mental response.

Throughout this book, the equal development of both sides of the body is stressed. Patterns and directions in space are also developed both clockwise and anticlockwise. Skaters, pianists, gymnasts, swimmers, have to work equally well on both sides of the body, to name a few. It makes the body more functional and coordinated but it does not necessarily mean the child will end up being ambidextrous.

This book has been written in a chronological way, and one long chapter is devoted to each of the three developmental stages outlined above. However, the same movement themes form the subheadings of each chapter to facilitate easy reference, as there is inevitably some overlap from one stage to the next. Despite the age-group being taught, if the teacher wishes to get an overview of development through the stages, the rationale behind choice and the timing of subject matter, it is recommended that she read all these chapters.

It will be seen that the chapter for the youngest stage is the shortest. This is because children in this group can't explore a theme as deeply or in as much detail as children two or three years older. Also very small children continually like to repeat games and stories (long after the adults in the group have become bored with them!) Unless these small children are given sufficient opportunity for repetition, they are robbed of their sense of achievement.

A note on size suitability of classes
Teachers are not always able to choose the number of children

they want to have in their classes, but the following numbers have been found to be suitable and manageable: age 2½ to 3½ ... between 6 and 10 children and at least half as many supportive adults; age 3½ to 4½ or 5 ... up to 12 children; age 4½ to 6 inclusive ... also up to 12 children (more if the teacher is imbued with a lot of energy). Within these attendance ranges there are enough children to create variety of response, and each child can receive adequate attention.

CHAPTER SIX

STAGE ONE—FROM ABOUT TWO AND A HALF TO THREE AND A HALF YEARS OLD

•General Description

> At the outset of mental evolution there is no dif-
> ferentiation between the self and the external
> world. . . . It follows that, because of this
> primitive lack of dissociation, everything that is
> perceived is centered on the subject's own ac-
> tivity.
>
> —Jean Piaget

> There was a child went forth every day;
> And the first object he look'd upon, that object
> he became;
> And that object became part of him for the day,
> or a certain part of the day, or for many years, or
> stretching cycles of years.
>
> —Walt Whitman

The child in this stage still feels the environment largely as a continuum of himself. For example, if a three year old were able to ar-
ticulate consciousness of the process of spinning round it would be
something like this:"My feet make everything go round me!",
rather than, "Look at me—I'm doing something called spinning
round and round."

N.B. Stories, Poems, and Games often occur within the context of
each chapter, and additional general purpose ones are given at the
end of each chapter.

In this stage of oneness with the environment, imitation of action is the key to teaching movement. Through imitation the child identifies with "the other" or "the teacher" out there, who thus becomes part of his continuum. In other words the child becomes what he beholds.

Imitating includes mimicking (e.g., copying the noise and motion of an airplane, the action of a pet rabbit, etc.). In view of the fact that children need to imitate movements before they can be truly creative with them, early dance teaching makes less use of images and more of concrete example. It starts with familiar actions and then gradually encompasses new ways of moving, building up the body-image bit by bit through direct physical experience.

Imitation, far from inhibiting the creative capacity, lays the foundations for its emergence later on.

Socially at this stage, children are *gradually* extending their awareness to all those who are around them. They first begin to get used to the other children in the dancing group by moving alongside each other. Sometimes they will stop and stare as if they were truly seeing each other for the first time. Shortly after "seeing" each other they derive great delight from holding hands and jumping together. They now have the joyful experience of their world overlapping with that of another.

When running a private class, a class for parent and child together is a valuable approach for this age group. The parent provides the child with one-to-one attention when it is needed, and imparts a sense of security in a new environment, bridging the gap between home and outside in what may well be a first group-learning experience. The parent often continues to dance with the child at home, and the dancing class therefore becomes a natural extension of everyday life.

Because parents are often busy working, Saturday mornings may be the best time to run a class of this type. Whether or not children attend with a parent or else dance, say, in a group at day-care with adult helpers, they will often spontaneously repeat their dance experiences at home. This develops their movement memory and, being in their own space, they will be more inclined to experiment with movement. Parents report that children spend many hours dancing at home and cannot wait for the next group session. In view

Encouragement from Mother

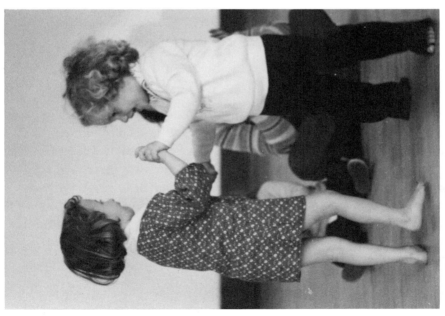

First dance together

of this and the fact that most little children in class reflect great
delight when they are moving, it seems that dancing fulfils a large
need in them.

It is interesting to note that children who have first danced in a
mixed child-adult group at two and a half, and then have gone on to
attend on their own at three and a half, seem to have more confidence, more listening ability and more tendency to produce their
own variations than most of the newcomers. Several times, children
have attended at the age of two and a half for a few months, and have
been fairly shy and inactive. At about four years old they have
returned at their own request, and clearly have remembered everything they learned (but did not express) when younger, only to express it now with much greater maturity and confidence.

In this, the youngest of the three preschool dance stages, it's important for the children to have a teacher who is informal, spontaneous, and is able to communicate her enjoyment of movement.
Dance is really a form of play and in the beginning should be
approached "lightly"!

Note on Format: In the following pages rather than having all
the directions in the third person, we will sometimes imagine that
we are talking to a class of preschoolers. These spoken sections will
be printed in *italics*.

•How to Begin

You will need to make a few brief opening remarks to let parents or
adult helpers know what is expected of them. It is good to tell them
that you hope they will join in the dancing as much as possible lend-
ing their encouragement and support, but to reassure them that it
doesn't matter if some children just want to watch to begin with.
You could point out that if a particular movement hasn't been
grasped, they can sometimes assist by gently moving a child's body
in the right way; however, enjoyment is essential and it is not worth
sacrificing enjoyment for accuracy at this point. They must judge
when and when not to intervene. Finally, if you wish to save your
immediate energies for teaching, request that they be responsible for
the physical welfare of the children as much as possible (blowing
noses, taking children to the bathroom, picking up someone who

has fallen over and giving him a hug, etc.).

The best way to get started is to ask everyone to come and sit in a circle on the floor. This formation limits the large space of the room and makes people feel they belong. It is useful to return to the circle whenever there is a need to draw attention back to a common focus.

•Circle Activities

The following circle activities can be interspersed throughout the class.

Rhythm Activities These are good as starters and can be carried out with the aid of an accompanist, with percussion, or with a record. About five minutes of rhythm activities at the beginning of a class usually suffice. Children will quite likely just stare at first. They will respond more to your action than to the words you use. They seem to like to do each action at least twice. It's best to introduce only one or two new actions at a time.

Let's all sit down—Can you clap like this! (Clapping at a walking pace)

Let's clap fast! (Clapping at a running pace)

Now let's tap our feet on the floor like this! (Alternate foot tapping).

We can do that faster and faster and then stop suddenly!

Shall we tap both feet together like this! (Resting body weight on hands)

Can you tap your hands and feet on the floor at the same time!

Let's shake our heads!

Now let's shake our hands!

How about lying on our backs and shaking our feet!

Let's sit up again. I wonder if you can tap your hands and feet and shake your heads all at once! (This is quite a challenge and is quite difficult)

Now let's kneel—that means getting on our knees like this. Do you think you can rock from side to side, like this!

Can you do a knee bounce? (Stationary "bouncing")

What about rocking backwards and forwards? Etc.

The above suggestions should be made when actually demonstrating the action—*not* before—as it is the picture which clarifies the words. Sometimes it's helpful to repeat the relevant verb over and over rhythmically while continuing the action. For example, "Bounce, bounce, bounce, bounce," while bouncing; or "Shake-shake-shake-shake-shake!" while shaking feet.

VARIATIONS:

You can provide sensory contrasts by speeding up and slowing down rhythm activities, by performing them first fast and then slowly, lightly then heavily, high in the air then low down near the floor.

You can perform the actions with an accompanying vocal *sound* (rather than word), and encourage the children to make the sound with you. For example, "Ch, ch, ch, ch," for alternate foot tapping; "Oooooooooooooooooh!" for head shaking; "Yumpi pumpi, yumpi pumpi," for rocking, etc.

As you do these activities, ideas such as the following may suddenly occur to you:

Can you bounce and clap at the same time?

Let's all stroke the air as if it were a pussy-cat!

Let's walk our fingers on the floor like a little fly going "walk, walk, walk, walk, walk," all over the place.

Embellishments and spontaneous additions are splendid as they keep everything alive and new, and prevent a dull routine from developing. Follow your good impulses, as this exemplifies one of the things you are teaching.

RATTLE BOXES

You may make a rattle box by placing a penny, dried peas, or any other "rattly" object inside an empty tin box or can. You then either tape on the lid or tape over the punched hole in the top. Sitting in the circle and shaking rattle boxes to the music is a much enjoyed, if deafening activity. A good follow up is to jump up and down, shaking the rattle box.

Generally speaking, children of this age seem to be able to rattle a box, clap or jump to a fairly fast regular beat (about twice a second) and keep in time. Gradually then learn to keep in time when going faster and slower than this.

Locating Different Parts of the Body

This is a suitable activity to follow up Rhythm Activities, while still in the circle. When a child lightly touches or taps different parts of his anatomy in turn, it helps to develop his body image through physical sensation. It's helpful to have a musical sound accompanying each action.

See how gently you can touch your hair—touch (both hands).

Can you find your ears? —touch

What about your nose?

Mouth? (Eyes, chest, tummy, knees, feet, shoulders, seat, neck, back, one elbow, the other elbow, fingers, etc.)

VARIATIONS:

Some of the above areas can be tapped to produce different percussive sounds (e.g., chests, heads, and tummies). Instead of using both hands, use first one and then the other, to further assist coordination.

At first, children respond slowly in finding the right part of their bodies, however as they become familiar with the routine, the exercise can be used to develop speed of response.

Now the idea can be taken further:

Let's touch our heads again—touch. Now let's do a head dance! (Rhythmic head movements, nodding, shaking from side to side, etc.)

Repeat with appropriate parts of the body—hands, back, shoulders, tummy, etc., but stay in the circle either sitting, kneeling, or standing, while doing the dances.

Locating different parts of the body (circle activity)

Training Speed of Response

(The next few circle activities are good to scatter throughout the class period.) Training speed of response clarifies body-mind connections. It brings a fuzzy awareness of a particular action into sharp focus through practice and will. A suitable movement game for developing speed of response at this stage is really a variation of Ring-around-a-Rosy, and is called *All Fall Down and All Stand Up!*:

Let's hold hands in the circle and we'll all jump round this way. Jump, jump, jump, jump, jump, jump, jump, jump, are you ready then? All Fall Down! (There should be 15 counts of suitable accompaniment ending with a crash.) *Now let's get up—very quickly! Let's fall down again—very quickly! Let's do that again. Now we'll jump in the circle the other way round* (repeat the procedure reversing the circle).

VARIATIONS:

It is helpful to pinpoint the sensation of speed by feeling the contrast of moving slowly. Thus, after falling down very quickly, you may vary the pace by getting up very slowly; conversely you may fall down very slowly and then get up again very quickly.

It's fun to say, "Aaaaaaaaaaaaaaaaah!" in a falling sound when falling, and in a rising sound when getting up again, stretching onto toes and reaching arms up into the air. You can do this either very slowly or very quickly.

Circle Game—Little Birds in the Nest

Let's all pretend we're in a great, big nest. Mommy Bird or Daddy Bird is in the nest with you and you're the Baby Bird. Now let's wake up and stretch our wings—Wheeeeeee—like that! What a lovely day it is. Let's walk to the edge of the nest and we'll all jump out and go flying together! Jump! (Flying action all round the room.) *Now it's time to come home again to the nest. Come on Baby Bird, let's all fly home again. Now we'll fold up our wings slowly, like this, and settle down again. Now Baby Bird is tired and is going to sleep for a while. Here's some sleepy music.* (Piano accompaniment, or just plain humming will do.)

It's time to wake up again. This time Mommy and Daddy Bird will stay in the nest and just Baby Bird will fly about, because Baby Bird knows how to fly now. Here we go! (Repeat without adults jointing in the flying...... you may have to accompany them, however, to get them out of the nest.)

VARIATION:

Little Frogs in the Pond; Little Mice in the Hole; Little Fish in the Sea; Little Snakes in the Grass, etc.

Our Own Dance in the Circle

As the children become more at home they enjoy dancing one by one in the middle of a sitting circle. Everyone else claps or taps or sways in time to the dance, for which it is useful to have instrumental and /or percussion accompaniment. At first, children often just want to jump! It's important not to pressure anyone who is reluctant to dance in the circle. Usually an extrovert child will lead the way for the rest, although it may take several weeks for everyone to want to have a turn. Sometimes, children may prefer to dance in the circle holding hands with another child. In this activity they learn as much from watching as from doing.

As well as giving children the opportunity to watch others, the circle dance gives them the satisfaction of having their own turn and individualized attention.

Singing in the Circle

(This seems to be a very satisfying way to finish a class.) Clapping, tapping, rocking to the rhythm, or miming the action of the song with the hands, are all good things to do along with the singing. Tunes must be fairly simple.

Suggested songs: *Rain Rain Go Away* (a three note song); *It's Raining, it's Pouring* (another three note song); *Twinkle Twinkle Little Star* (a song with a lot of notes "next-door" to each other); *The Bear went over the Mountain* (Another one with next-door notes).

Children will go on singing the songs they have learned when they get home. It's important for the teacher to be able to sing in tune, as children, with their strong ability to imitate, will otherwise copy out of tune. On this subject Shinichi Suzuki has this to say, in his book *Nurtured by Love*: . . . a baby absorbs perfectly any out-of-tune pitch of its mother's lullabies. It has a marvelous ear. That's why the child will later sing in the same way. . . . Thus, if we wanted to, we could make all children throughout the world tone-deaf." If you feel you can't sing in tune well enough—use a record.

The switch from movement to singing at the end of the class seems a natural one, and children enjoy it. After all, many subjects naturally overlap (singing, dancing, poetry, and music are all very compatible as they each contain the element of rhythm). It's only rigid educational tradition that tends to keep different "subjects" in water-tight compartments.

•Using the Space of the Whole Room

When moving away from the circle for the first time, do so gradually and not all at once, or else a few children may remain rooted to the spot.

When jumping, galloping, running, etc., the tempo of the music should be geared to the children rather than to adults. In general, children require a faster tempo for locomotor movements because of their smaller bodies.

Clapping or percussion accompaniment plus musical instrument or record, are desirable for the following activities:

Let's all jump! (Jumping on the spot and gradually spreading out into the room)

Let's jump and clap our hands.

Now let's do another dance called a gallop.

Now let's play a game called STOP!

It's useful to teach the children that an extra large bang on the tambourine (or other consistent sound) means STOP wherever they are. Make a game of learning how to do it by signalling STOP in unexpected places, in the middle of a jumping or galloping dance. Learning how to STOP gives the children a focus of concentration and the opportunity to listen for the next activity. It also helps to train speed of response.

Shall we do a running dance? (A quick, wide-legged run hopping from one foot to the other with knees lifted, is the typical way children of this age run.)

Can you turn around like this? (A walking spin on the spot with arms out to the sides. An adult will probably have to help with this one at first.) *Now let's turn around the other way.*

Help will certainly be needed in reversing, as little children will otherwise turn round and round in one direction (usually anticlockwise) until they fall over! By the same token it is a useful sensory exercise to *let* them turn one way until giddy—which they seem to enjoy—and then they should experience the sensation again of turning first one way, then the other, when the unwinding action prevents most of the giddiness.

The above are just a few of the easier "standing up" dances. The following ones involve beginning from a different base position.

•On the Floor Dances

An *on the floor* dance is one in which a major part of the body (excluding just the feet) is in contact with the floor during movement. For example, one can dance sitting down and moving along. These *on the floor* dances are a useful follow up to the preceding jumping, galloping, running, and turning dances.

Can you do a sitting down dance like this? (Walking on the seat, heels, and hands with bent knees)

Let's get on our tummies and move like wiggly worms.

Perhaps we can go for a dance on our backs. (Lying on the back and sliding backwards by pushing off first from one foot and then the other. Some abdominal strength is needed, and help may be required at first.)

Shall we roll over and over like this?

Can we do a dance on our knees? (Walking or bounding on the knees, or crawling on hands and knees.)

Now how about a dance on our hands and feet? (Walking along like a bear)

VARIATIONS:

It's possible to go around in a *circle* on the floor in any of the above basic positions. Remember to reverse the turns.

ANIMALS

One very popular way of dancing "on the floor" is to mimic *animals,* as in the case of the wiggly worm or the bear. A picture book containing good illustrations of the animals is always popular and acts as a movement stimulus. Some examples are: *Fish*—rolling slowly from side to side; *Snakes*—slithering on tummies; *Crocodiles*—on tummies with the head held up, and pushing along on both hands with the body dragging behind; *Mice*—shuffling on hands and knees; *Lions*—creeping on hands and feet, followed by running in this position; *Frogs*—jumping from crouched position on hands and feet; *Ducks*—waddling on feet in crouched position; *Monkeys*—running in a bent back position, swinging arms; *Giraffes*—striding with stretched necks; *Birds*—swaying with arms slowly waving up and down; *Crabs*—walking on hands and feet with tummy uppermost; etc. When mimicking these creatures, encourage roaring, hissing, squeaking, growling, etc., as appropriate.

Children may need help in finding the right starting position, or else they may end up like the little girl who, trying to move forward on her hands and knees like a mouse, had her head pressed firmly against the floor in front of her, and wailed "I can't move—my head's too long!"

FREE DANCE

After the children have done some standing up dances followed by some on the floor dances it's a good thing to let them have a *"free"* dance in which they do any movements they like. With adults now improvising along with them and encouraging experimentation, they may choose to copy first one, then another. This extends their sources of imitation, opening up their field of choice. Eventually they will initiate movements for themselves, drawing on those with which they are familiar. Finally, they will

Bears

Free dance

find new ways of moving for themselves from time to time. When they frequently create new variations, they are ready for the next stage, whatever their age.

This "free" dance can be quite a long one and frequently starts with adult and child interacting—creeping round each other, rolling side by side, climbing over each other, or jumping together holding hands. Different pieces of music can be played with varying rhythms, tempos, and moods. Sometimes a child will sit and watch for a while, and if he gets tired he may even just curl up and close his eyes.

After a while, the children will welcome a quiet, lying down piece of music. They will often rock from side to side or kick their legs as they listen.

•Sensory Contrasts

In order to develop different qualities of movement it is necessary to introduce sensory contrasts. For example: big and small; fast and slow; light and heavy; floppy and stiff, etc. By defining extreme contrasts in movement at first—for example by moving very lightly like a snowflake and then very heavily like an elephant—one gradually is able to become aware of more subtle contrasts and nuances in quality of movement. Likewise, as the body is our channel for understanding the world, the greater the differentiation in movement the more sensory contrasts will be recognized in our environment.

Some contrasts may be explored by moving from one extreme through to the other. For example, it's possible to move continuously from a very small shape to a very big one, from a very fast pace to a very slow one, etc. It is not so easy, however, to move continuously through a series of very light to very heavy movements or through very floppy to very stiff ones, because to do so requires much greater muscular control.

After a while it is possible to combine different contrasts which seem to work together well. For example, little children can move both lightly and quickly, slowly and heavily, floppily and quickly *or* floppily and slowly. However, to move both quickly and heavily is difficult because it requires more force than a very small body can easily generate.

Activities focusing on sensory contrasts are an important part of every dance class. You need not work on a lot of contrasts in any given week. It seems best to spread them out and to repeat them frequently. Working with stories and poems is another opportunity to bring out contrasts.

Images to encourage contrasts may be used when appropriate. As this age group often finds it difficult just to visualize images based on words, a picture or an object brought to class to illustrate the subject to be danced, gives a visible stimulus. For example, a straight stick, and a floppy pillow brought to class, passed round, and handled, will be far more conducive to making stiff and floppy movements than just talking about a stick and a pillow would. Again, a picture of a little flower beside a big tree, will be more evocative than a mere description. Many objects used to illustrate movements tend to express more than one sensory characteristic at the same time. For example, a dropped feather moves *lightly* and *slowly*. This is all to the good; the child will absorb the qualities through watching, and express them through imitation.

The following are examples of how to work on different sensory contrasts.

Tempo

Let's move our whole self very, very fast like this! (Stamping feet, shaking arms, wiggling the entire body)
Now let's lie down and see how slowly we can roll over and over.

See if you can sit up gently and slowly like this, and rock from side to side very slowly. It makes you feel sleepy doesn't it? Let's close our eyes and go on rocking for a while.

Now, we'll open our eyes and start tapping our hands slowly on the floor like the rain coming down. We'll get faster and faster. Now we're getting slower and slower again. The rain is just going pit pat pit pat pit pat ... oh, now it's stopped!

This time let's stand up and move like a train starting off slowly and getting faster and faster. Cha cha, cha cha, cha cha, cha cha, chhhhhhhhhhhhhh!

Suitable objects to bring to class to demonstrate differing tempos would be: An *eggbeater*—first beaten very slowly and gradually speeding up . . . . . . The action could be arms reaching down in front and making slow circles out and round, and gradually increasing in speed. *A wind-up clockwork toy*—In this case the toy starts off fast and then slows down. The children can pretend to wind themselves up and then mimic the toy. *An umbrella*—this could be opened and closed slowly, then opened and closed fast. The children could mime this action with either their arms (standing up), their legs (sitting down), or their whole body (curling head and back to legs, and back again—either standing or lying).

Here are two stories based on the idea of moving fast and moving slowly:

THE SCARED BEAR

Bear wanted to go for a walk. It was a hot day so he walked slowly through the woods, like this (on hands and feet). *Bear came to the river. He swam slowly through the river, like this* (slithering on tummies). *Then Bear shook himself slowly. After a bit Bear came to the hill. He walked slowly up the hill, like this* (lifting hands and feet high). *At the top of the hill was a wall. Bear came to the wall and stood up slowly, like this. Bear looked over the top . . . . . . and there was a person looking at him!*

Bear stared at the person and the person stared at Bear. Bear was scared and stood quite, quite still—long enough for the person to count to five—one, two, three, four, five.

Then Bear moved very quickly! He jumped down from the wall very quickly, like this. He ran down the hill so quickly that he fell down and rolled over and over into the river—SPLASH! He swam across the river very quickly, like this. He scrambled out and shook himself very quickly. He ran very quickly through the woods, like this . . . . . . Then he slowed down again because it was a hot day.

Bear lay under a tree in the shade like this, panting . . . . . . and thinking . . . . . . "That person looked like a friendly person—I was silly to be such a scared Bear!" Then, because it was such a hot day, he curled up slowly, like this, and went to sleep.

MRS. FAST

There was once a lady called Mrs. Fast, who did everything oh so quickly! When she was lying in the bed in the morning she woke up—oh so quickly, and sat up just like this, and jumped out of bed—oh so quickly, and put on her clothes very very very very fast. That's why she was called Mrs. Fast.

She rushed into the bathroom and washed her face and hands—oh so quickly. She cleaned her teeth, scrub, scrub, scrub, very very fast. She ran down the stairs and opened the fridge—oh so quickly. She poured some juice and swallowed it down, gulp, gulp, gulp, gulp, gulp, very very fast. She gobbled some bread and butter and honey—gobble, gobble, gobble, gobble, gobble—oh so quickly. And she didn't stop to wash the dishes. She opened the door and ran down the path very very fast. She went on running down the road—oh so quickly—run, run, run, run, run, run, run— just as fast as she could go, and she didn't look where she was going. Suddenly—BIM BAM WALLOP! Mrs. Fast fell over! She had slipped on a piece of orange peel.

Mrs. Fast didn't know what had happened. She lay there quite still for a whole minute. Then she sat up—oh so slowly, and she shook her head. Then she stood up—oh so slowly, and moved her hands and her arms and her shoulders and her back and her legs—oh so slowly, to see if they still worked. Then she started to walk home very very slowly. She went up the path very very slowly. She opened her door very very slowly. And still wondering what had happened, she went up the stairs—oh so slowly—to bed. She didn't even bother to take off her clothes. She lay down very slowly indeed and went to sleep.

In a little while she woke up and she got out of bed, not too fast, and not goo slow, but just like you would. Then she said, 'I'd better go to work now.'' And she went down stairs, not too fast and not too slow—but just like you would, and out through the door and down the path—just like you would. And she walked down the road, not too fast and not too slow—just like you would, and went all the way to work.

But do you know, the next morning when Mrs. Fast woke up, she had forgotten all about the orange peel. And she sat up—oh so quickly! And she jumped out of bed—oh so quickly! Then she

*cleaned her teeth, scrub, scrub, scrub, scrub, scrub, scrub, very very
fast. Then she washed her hands and face just as fast as she
could—because that's why she was called Mrs. Fast. Then she went
down stairs very very fast and she opened the door of the fridge just
as quickly as she could. She got out the orange juice and she gulped
it down—gulp, gulp, gulp, gulp, gulp—oh so quickly. Then she ate
her bread and butter and honey, gobble, gobble, gobble, gobble,
gobble, gobble, very very fast. She didn't stop to wash up again and
she ran out of the front door and down the path, just as quickly as
she could. Then she went on running down the road—oh so quickly—run, run, run, run, run! And do you know, I think she's running
still!*

N.B. It can be seen from the above stories that it is really only
necessary to memorize their simple outline and then the details can
be filled in on the spot. It's far better to do this than to squint at a
script every sentence or two and hold up the action.

Weight

*Let's all go tippy-toe very lightly all over the place, so nobody can
hear us. Can you hear me when I go tippy-toe?*

*Now let's go thump thump thump all over the floor on our hands
and feet like a big elephant pushing into the floor.*

*Now we'll touch our fingers together lightly and gently. Can you
just feel your finger-tips? Now touch the floor lightly and gently.*

*Have you ever seen bubbles floating in your bath? Let's move this
finger lightly like a floating bubble. Shall we make all our fingers
wriggle lightly about like lots of new bubbles?*

*Let's kneel up and push down into the floor very hard, with our
hands in front of us. Push . . . . . . and up. Push . . . . . . and up.
Push . . . . . . and up.* (This is one of the few movements in which a
small light child can achieve a sense of power and weight.)

The following objects can help children understand the sense of
weight: *A fluffy cottonball*—Pass around the ball, letting each child
hold it lightly in his hands. Then give each child a piece to himself
and let him throw it in the air, pick it up off the ground and throw it
up again. *A sack of potatoes*—Demonstrate its weight by dragging it
along, then get the others to do the same. Each child can then go

heavy and floppy like a sack of potatoes and an adult can drag him along.

Size and Contracting and Expanding

Let's make ourselves just as small as we can. Can you curl up so that you're as small as a little mouse? Now can you move about in that tiny mouse way?

How big can you make yourself? That's right you can stretch right up with your hands above your head. Can you walk like that?

Now we'll curl up small again. This time let's slowly grow bigger and bigger on the floor like a big pool of water. Are you all stretched out like this?

Can you make yourself all small and bent over, standing up? Now can you grow fatter and fatter? Now let's grow all small and bent again.

A *rubber band*—stretching a rubber band and letting it slowly shrink back again can help the children understand the idea of expanding and contracting. Then they can stretch out and shrink back again themselves, using their arms and chests and stretching sideways. *Play-dough*—can be flattened out and then rolled into a ball again, and the children can do this with their bodies, lying on the floor.

Degree of Tension in the Body

Can you make yourself all stiff? Can you make your arms and legs and back straight and stiff like this? Now let's walk about like stiff wooden dolls.

Can you make yourself go all floppy now? Let's make our arms and legs and shoulders and backs and all the rest of us go flop flop flop all over the place. Let's do a floppy dance like that to some floppy music!

A pair of *scissors*—can demonstrate a stiff out and in action and then this can be imitated with arms and legs. A *Raggedy Ann*—can show how a limp object can flop. The children can then go so floppy that they fall in a heap.

Levels

How far can you reach up—right up to the ceiling! Let's jump and get higher up still. Now let's do a high dance. (If possible accompany with high music.) *How near to the floor can you get! Can you reach your whole self down to the floor! Is any bit of you left sticking up in the air! Is your head down there too! Now let's do a dance way down here.* (Low music if possible.)

Up and down movement games can also assist in training musical pitch.

THE BEAR AND THE HONEY

If you have a piano or other instrument available, ask the accompanist to play a very high note. The children respond by reaching up above their heads and standing on tip-toe like a bear who is reaching honey out of a tree. Ask the accompanist to play a very low note—now the children crouch down at the bottom of the tree. The same high and low notes should then be played in random order, with pauses between them to allow the children to assume a high or low position. Most children below three and a half cannot differentiate pitch at first.

A picture of an airplane or a toy airplane can be shown to the class, and then a game of airplanes can follow, moving through low, medium, and high levels, dipping, climbing, and wheeling around.

Sensory Combinations

TREE

Let's pretend we're growing like a tree. Here it is just sticking up out of the earth. Slowly it grows big and tall. Now the branches slowly grow out sideways. Here comes the wind. It slowly blows the big, heavy branches. Now the little leaves at the end of the branches are quickly shaking very lightly all around. The wind goes away. The tree is still again.

SNOWMAN

(Only use this idea in a snowy climate!) *Let's stand like a snowman. The sun is shining and the snow-man gets very hot and starts to*

• Rolling

Levels
• Growing up tall

melt. It gets smaller and smaller like this. First our heads, then our shoulders, then our backs, then our knees go all loose and heavy and slowly flop down to the floor. There you are, all in a heap and quite, quite still.

FEATHER

Look, I'm going to drop this feather. See it lightly, slowly floating down! Let's do that with our hands and arms and all of ourselves
—down, down, down to the floor, lightly from side to side.

MUSHROOMS AND ROCKS

(This game was introduced by a substitute teacher and the origin of it is unknown to the author. It is a very good way to become aware of tension and relaxation.)

Have you ever seen a mushroom growing in the earth? Mushrooms fall over very easily when they are pushed. I'm going to curl up like a mushroom, on my knees with my head down, like this. Now, will a grown up please come and give me a push. Oh . . . . . . see how easily I fall over . . . . . . I go all floppy and light just like a mushroom. Now this grown up will curl up and I'll try and push her over. Watch. See if you can do it now —tuck your knees up under you. Now we'll try to push you over. Over you roll, all light and floppy. That's good. Now see if you can push us grown-ups over.

(In two or three weeks when the Mushroom idea is well established you can introduce the idea of Rocks.)

Here's a picture of a big strong rock. It would be difficult to push that over wouldn't it? Now I'm going to pretend to be a rock. Watch me curl up. Now I'm all stiff and strong and heavy. Would someone like to try and push me over? Thank you. Oh . . . . . . I'm stuck here— I won't roll over because I'm too stiff and strong and heavy like a rock. Can you make yourself like a rock so a grown-up can't push you over? Now see if a grown-up can do it while you try and push them over.

Shall we pretend to be a mushroom again now, so we can go all light and floppy again!

The above exercises in sensory contrasts may be too advanced for your class for some time. Towards the end of the year, however, the ideas should be useable.

Space

Body Shape

At this point in child development it's best to encourage the "feeling" of certain shapes and patterns without making an abstract concept of them. In other words it would be more suitable for you to stretch your body into a long line and say, "Let's do this," than to say, "This is a straight line. Now *you* get into a straight line." Copying is once more the key to doing, and "forcing" of concept must be avoided as it leads to dimunition of feeling.

Some *body shapes* with which to experiment are: curled, stretched, humped, flattened, twisted, straightened. For example, you can curl while on your back, side or front, or else while crouched and balanced on your feet. You can stretch wide while standing or lying on the floor on your front or back. Pictures and objects brought to class are once more very helpful. A twisted plastic bag tie, or a picture of a caterpillar humping are two suitable examples.

Floor Patterns

Children of two and three years old will make random *floor patterns* in space unless any other way is suggested. If the whole group moves together, adults seem to choose to move in an anti-clockwise direction, and the children sometimes follow and sometimes dart around them like puppies going for a walk.

Children this age can move in *circles on the spot* from standing, kneeling, sitting, and lying positions. They can move in a *group circle* holding hands such as in the All Fall Down and All Stand Up game. They can also move *down the room in a straight line*, if they are first positioned in a line, side by side with their backs to a wall, and if you lead them with your back to them. A game in this formation is called, "Crossing the Bridge."

CROSSING THE BRIDGE

Let's play a game called "Crossing the Bridge." Let's pretend this is a big, wide bridge. (Show them a picture of a bridge.) *The bridge is between you and the wall over there. I'm going to cross the bridge in front of you and you all follow me in* this *way.* (Lead "across the bridge" with a simple movement, say, jumping. The children follow across behind you.) *Let's all cross back again.* (Choose a different movement, say, crawling on hands and knees.) *And now one of your mommies can go in front.* (Mother leads with a different movement.) *Now we'll go over the bridge again. Would one of* you *like to go in front?* (It's quite normal for no one to volunteer—most of the children still want a model to copy. If one of the more mature ones leads across it is likely he will remember and copy what has just gone before. If there are no child volunteers you and the other parents or grown-ups can find many different ways of "Crossing the Bridge" for the children to follow.)

Children can move towards a focal point and away from it again if they begin in a circle and move *into the center and out again.* This is a good way of learning to move backwards. One way of doing this is to turn the exercise into a game. You can stand in the middle of the circle and say:

Can you jump all the way to me? Now can you tip-toe all the way back? Can you creep to me on your hands and feet just as quickly as you can? Can you crawl backwards, now, while you watch me? etc. (The Spider and the Fly story, near the end of this chapter, gives good examples of moving in and out of a circle in this way.)

These are enough patterns for a child of this age to cope with.

•Props

Props provide variety and interest and can illustrate a number of movement themes. The following props have been found to be useful. More will no doubt come to mind.

SCARVES

A light chiffon scarf held at one corner can be made to "dance" in a variety of ways. Provide suitable "floaty" music and let the children move in any way they please, with the aim of making the scarf really move. Eventually, with the other adults and yourself as copying models, children will dance their scarves in many different ways—round and round, up and down, wiggling them from side to side, spinning around with the scarves trailing behind them, shaking them, running with the scarf streaming behind, "swooshing" the scarf from side to side, etc. At some suitable point, stop the music and ask the children to hold the scarf in the *other* hand. Repeat the scarf dance. Later on ask the children to hold the scarf in *both* hands, while they dance.

Extended arm movements should be encouraged. Scarf dances are best discovered "on the spot" at first, and later may be done jumping or running round the room. The scarf dance is an example of a *light* dance.

HOOPS

A light plastic hoop may be held between two children with both pairs of hands on the hoop. At first, children usually like to hold the outside of the hoop facing each other. The children then find their own movement variations to a suitable piece of music.

If the children are nearer two and a half than three and a half, they will probably prefer to do the hoop dance with mother or father or another adult first. Climbing in and out of the hoop while the grown-up holds it, rocking the hoop, or jumping with it are all popular activities.

When a hoop is given to each child and laid on the floor, a dance can be done "inside" the hoop, and then "outside" the hoop (e.g., running around it first one way and then the other); show them how to do it first. Then a dance can be done jumping in and out, over the rim and back again. These simple activities will aid in extending the child's feeling for using space in different ways.

MATS

A light mat can be used as a "boat." Sitting on the "boat", hold the edges and rock from side to side while singing "Row, Row, Row your Boat." The boat can also be held and rocked upon while kneel-

Scarves

ing, crouching, or lying on it, singing all the while. A dance can then be done on top of the boat, or one can "swim" all around between the mats.

A light mat may also make a good snail shell as the children shuffle along on their knees holding their "house" on their backs, and practicing slow movement.

A HAND PUPPET

Children seem very eager to imitate a puppet, particularly when it also "speaks" to them, suggesting what they do.

OTHER TOYS

Quite often a child will bring a toy to class because he is fond of it and wants it for company. If the child is willing to lend it to you, it may well provide a good impromptu movement stimulus. The following toys have been brought to my classes: A Raggedy Ann; a stuffed, knitted caterpillar; a hinged wooden dog; a picture book; a racing car; a mouth organ, and a teddy bear.

You may wish to bring a bag full of toys yourself and have a Grab Bag game. This consists of asking children in turn to close their eyes and to pull one of the toys out of the bag. The toy's movement possibilities are then explored and mimicked.

PARENTS

Adults can turn themselves into suitable props by creating "tunnel" shapes with their bodies, either by straddling their legs, by making archways with their hands and feet on the floor with either their seats or tummies towards the ceiling, by making sideways tunnels between an arm and the floor, or in any other way. The children then go through all the tunnels they can find, one after the other, to musical accompaniment.

This activity helps children to begin to move independently of their parents or adult helpers. A shy child may gain the courage to leave the side of his parent for the first time.

•Listening

When the class has been very noisy and lively, it's sometimes useful to play a listening game. Gather everyone into a circle and ask them to close their eyes. Tell them that when you say, "Go!" they are just to listen without making any noise. Tell them that in a minute you will say, "Stop!" at which point they will open their eyes and tell you what they have heard.

Don't be surprised if they hear as many imaginary noises as real ones! A class of children over six years old will usually only mention objective sounds, such as, "a car going by" . . . "a door slamming" . . . or "a fly buzzing about." Little children will just as likely say, "I heard a cow" . . . "I heard my Daddy singing" . . . "I heard splash splash splash in the bath"; whereupon the other children are likely to copy and say, "*I* heard a cow", "I heard *my* Daddy", etc. It's hard to say if they know they have imagined these sounds, but in any event it seems best not to try to differentiate them from "real" sounds, but to acknowledge what they say they have heard with interest. The object of quietening the group and creating a still, listening focus will have been achieved whether they have heard the rain on the roof or a lion inside their heads!

•Doing and Listening

The following is an exercise which helps to develop movement memory if the child is ready to do so, by associating a certain musical sound with a nature image and a particular way of moving. The remembering is not likely to be clear and vivid at first, and may be barely conscious. Whether the child recalls the movement or not, the "listening" part provides a restful interlude.

It's important that the mood and rhythm of the music to accompany each nature image can be repeated. For example, if percussion and voice are used in this exercise, a single strong drum beat might be used (and later repeated) for the sun; a "dotted" rhythm on the triangle for rocking the moon; shaking of hand bells for the star; a "shhhhhhh" sound made by the voice for the wind; a tambourine rattle for the rain, and a series of fast loud beats on the drum or tambourine for the thunder. As it is hard to illustrate the movement and play percussion instruments at the same time, the help of other adults could be enlisted for the latter. *It's best not to have more than two or three variations at one time*, or else the child's memory will become jumbled. This activity is more suited to children of nearly three and a half years old, than to younger ones.

SKY AND EARTH DANCE

This is the sun —
Let's lift it high across the sky
And walk so slowly. (Slow, solemn walk bending knees as in a native Indian dance.)

This is the moon —
Let's rock it here, let's rock it there
Oh so gently. (Hands held above heads and upper body swaying from side to side.)

This is a star —
Let's twinkle twinkle all around
Oh so lightly. (Shaking hands and head and body while turning on the spot.)

This is the wind —
Let's swish about and swoosh about
Oh so wildly. (Swinging arms from side to side across body while rocking from foot to foot.)

This is the rain —
Let's patter down and pitter down
Oh so quickly. (Running on the spot while wriggling fingers.)

This is the thunder —
Let's crash about and thump about
Oh so strongly. (Big crouching jumps all over the place and banging of palms on the floor.)

This is me —
Let's all lie down and close our eyes
And be quite still. (Slowly sinking to the floor and lying quietly.)

Now . . . . . . Let's listen to the sun (Sun sound).
              Let's listen to the moon (Moon sound), etc.

(When all the sounds have been played back)—
This is me —
Let's open eyes and all stand up
And jump about. (Carefree release from concentration.)

It doesn't matter if the children don't understand all the words, because they will get a feeling for them as they move according to the visual demonstration.

•More stories, Poems and Games

THE DRAGON WHO WANTED A FRIEND

Once upon a time there was a Dragon who lived in a hole in the ground. The Dragon was very very sad because he had no friends to play with. So one day, the Dragon thought he would try to find a friend. He crawled out of his hole in the ground and went off down the hill, thump, thump, thump, thump, thump.

The first thing the Dragon saw, standing in the green field, was a Horse. The Dragon said, "Horse, will you play with me?" But the Horse said, "Oh, no!" and galloped away just as fast as he could go. So the Dragon went on a bit further, thump, thump, thump, thump, thump.

The next thing the Dragon saw, sitting on a grey rock, was a Frog. The Dragon said, "Frog, will you play with me?" But the Frog said, "Oh, no!" and hopped away just as fast as he could go. So the Dragon went on a bit further, thump, thump, thump, thump, thump.

The next thing the Dragon saw, sitting on a pink flower, was a Butterfly. The Dragon said, "Butterfly, will you play with me?" But the Butterfly said, "Oh, no!" and flew away just as fast as she could go. So the Dragon went on a bit further, thump, thump, thump, thump, thump.

Well the next thing the Dragon saw, creeping out of the black forest, was a Lion. The Dragon said, "Lion, will you play with me?" But the Lion said, "Oh, no!" and ran away just as fast as he could go. So the Dragon went on a bit further, Thump, thump, thump, thump, **thump.**

New the next thing the Dragon saw, sliding in the green grass, was a Snake. The Dragon said, "Snake, will you play with me?" But the Snake said, "Oh, no!" and wiggled away just as fast as she could go.

Poor Dragon! He was now feeling very sad indeed, so he just sat down and began to cry, like this, "Oooooohooooohoooo!" Can you *make that noise? "Oooohoooohooohoooohooohoooohooo!" He made such a big noise that all the other Dragons who were living round about came to see what was the matter. When the Dragon looked up there were one, two, three, four, five, six, seven, eight, nine, ten Dragons all sitting round him. He* was surprised. *The Dragon said, "Will* you *play with me?"*

And all the other Dragons said, "Yes, of course!" So they all rolled over and over and over in a happy Dragon dance. After that they all *went to live in the hole in the ground, and the Dragon wasn't lonely any more.*

THE SPIDER AND THE FLY

Once there was a spider who was fast asleep in a crack. One day when the sun came out she crept out of the crack and stretched all of her legs, like this. Then, she said, "I want some dinner. I'm hungry! I will make a web to catch a fly." So she started to make a web and crept round and round and round and round, spinning the web behind her. Round and round and round and round she went. Then when she had finished, she rested in the corner of her web, and went to sleep.

Just then, a fly came buzzing by like this, "BZZZZZZZZ!" and it buzzed all over the place. Up and down, side to side, round and round, until at last it flew straight into the web. ......G-Doing! Help! the fly was stuck.

The fly woggled and wiggled and wiggled and woggled; he jiggled and joggled and joggled and jiggled—but he was still stuck. He tried to jump—he tried to jump again; he tried to pull back-

wards out of the web—back, back, back, back, back ...... but the web pulled him forwards again—forwards, forwards, forwards, forwards, forwards. And he pulled back, back, back, back, back, and the sticky web pulled him forwards yet again—forwards, forwards, forwards, forwards, forwards. So the fly was still stuck. He stayed quite still for a minute wondering what to do.

Well—the spider woke up, and crept towards the fly like this. Did you know that spiders could jump? Well they can, they jump this way, watch! ...... JUMP! Let's all do that ...... JUMP! We'll do it again ...... So the spider crept towards the fly and gave a great big jump. But the fly gave an extra big jiggle and got out just in time! Let's give an extra big jiggle ...... JIGGLE! Out flew the fly, feeling all sticky! BZZZZZZZZZZZZZZZZZZZ!And he never came back again.

Just then the wind came blowing like this ...... WHOOOOOOOOOOOOOOOO! And it tore the spider's web in two. WHOOOOOOOOOOOOOOOO! went the wind again, and the web floated like this in two pieces!

The spider felt very cross. She said, "I must make another web because I am very hungry and I want my dinner very much." So she began to make another web to catch another fly. And she crept round and round and round and round and round and round and round and round, until she had finished. Then she crept into the corner—waiting for another fly. But this time she didn't go to sleep. Do you think she caught one?

The following two poems bring in the use of vocalized sounds. Try and encourage the children to make the sounds along with you so they can enjoy accompanying *themselves*.

BONFIRE

This is the way the bonfire's lit
Tch Tch Tch (Mime action of lighting fire with a match—include your standard match warning)

This is the way the flames begin
Tsssssssssssssss (Wriggling)

This is the way the smoke comes out
Haaaaaaaaaaaaaaa (Waving whole body slowly)

This is the way the flames grow big
Whooo Whooo Whooo (Leaping with "Stationary" feet!)

This is the way the sparks jump out
K K K (Jumping outwards from a crouching position)

This is the way the fire goes down
Feeeee Fooooo (Sinking, shrinking action)

This is the way the log rolls over
Yoinga Yoinga Yoinga (Heavy slow rolling)

And that's *the end of the fire!*

LEAF DANCE

I'm a leaf, can't you see
Falling, falling, look at me!
Mmmmmmmmmmmmmmmm!
I'm a leaf, blowing high,
See me right up in the sky!
Wheeeeeeeeeeeeeee!

I'm a leaf, down so low,
Rolling over, Watch me go!
Yumpity Yumpity Yumpity Yumpity Yum

I'm a leaf in a heap . . . . . .
Now I think I'll go to sleep!
Shhhhhhhhhhhhhhh!

As with the stories, if the words are too hard at first, much of the action will be comprehended nonverbally.

HOUSE AND GARDEN

This is a movement game which mimics the actions of grown-ups looking after the house and garden. Small children strongly relate to houses for they represent security and are one of the first things they try to draw. In this age of mechanization, when many tasks which previously required manual labour are accomplished through pushing buttons, there are fewer and fewer traditional tasks to copy. But those which are still relevant such as digging in the garden, painting the kitchen, washing the windows— make good movement material, as the children are already familiar with the actions.

A possible approach is to pretend you have a house and garden right there which everyone is trying to make as bright and beautiful as possible.

•Dividing the Material into Lessons

Bearing in mind the amount of repetition desired by two and a half to three and a half year olds, the preceding chapter contains enough dance activities and suggestions for a whole year, with one or two half hour classes per week. Whatever the total number of classes taught, half an hour seems the optimum time span for a class this age.

An appropriate half hour dance plan could be:
Rhythm activities
Locating different parts of the body
Activities using space of whole room
"On the Floor" dances
Sensory contrast activity and /or "Prop" activity
Use of space activity and /or Listening practice
A story, poem, or game
A song

It will be seen that if equal time were given to each activity, there would be a change of subject approximately every three minutes. In practice, it doesn't work out this way as, naturally, when concentration is good, fewer activities will be covered than on other days. It's best if each activity is done as long as attention warrants it, and that a very flexible approach towards the plan is maintained. It's much more important to keep the children interested and happy than to fuss about what is written down on a piece of paper.

This is not to underrate the usefulness of a plan, but to set it in its right perspective—as a guide rather than a dictator.

CHAPTER SEVEN

STAGE TWO—FROM ABOUT THREE AND A HALF TO FOUR AND A HALF OR FIVE YEARS OLD

•General Description

> *Who would ever imagine that the needless assistance given to a child is the first of the various repressions which he will experience and one which can have serious consequences in later life?*
>
> —*Maria Montessori*

> *I never did, I never did, I never did like*
>   *"Now take care, dear!"*
> *I never did, I never did, I never did want*
>   *"Hold my hand";*
> *I never did, I never did, I never did think much of*
>   *"Not up there, dear!"*
> *It's no good saying it. They don't understand.*
>
> —*A.A. Milne*

At this stage, most children have a growing sense of themselves as individuals. They *interact* with their environment rather than merge with it. Because of this they increasingly want to create their own ways of doing things. While the desire to imitate is still fairly strong, the desire to innovate is even stronger.

Autonomy can be encouraged by giving an example of a certain type of movement, and then by asking the children to make up variations. For example, "Let's do a very light dance like this with our feet," (example given), can be followed with "Now can *you* do a very light dance with your hands?" (no example given). At this point some children may crouch down and pat the floor lightly with their hands and fingers, others may lightly flop their hands in the air while still others may make up a special movement. There will always be some who watch what the others do first and then imitate. The strongest personalities inevitably turn into leaders and, therefore, the more hesitant, timid ones should be encouraged in their original efforts so that they may also eventually give examples to the rest of the class. Gradually, the children in this age group learn to interact with each other far more than those in the preceding one.

In private dance classes, most children at this stage benefit from *not* having a parent present in the room with them. They are freer to participate when their attention is no longer being channelled towards the parent in either a request for support, or a desire to rebel. If the dance class is part of a day-care center, preschool, or kindergarten setting, the problem of parents being present will not arise. However, if a private dancing class is being held to which the parent specially brings the child, about ten per cent are not ready for their parent to leave at the beginning of the first class. If these ten per cent are left on their own they become fearful or tearful, and upset others as well.

The best way to forestall this seems to be a brief word with the parents just before the first class, suggesting they should leave if possible—but that if they feel their child needs them there for emotional support, to stay until enough confidence has been built up. Most parents are very sensible and cooperative. They may either join in or sit and watch, but their child should be told beforehand when they are going to leave, as parents who creep off can cause a trauma which may last for weeks. It's important to try not to confuse the behavior of a child who is moderately timid and just wants to watch at first, with that of a child who feels really threatened.

Generally, everything sorts itself out in two or three weeks as long as no child is unduly pressured.

This is the age and stage when the unique but malleable personality of each child can grow through learning to move in many different ways. The shy child may learn the pleasure of leaping; the aggressive one may discover enjoyment in gentle, delicate movements; the over active child may learn to move slowly like a drifting fog; and the placid child may get excited when dancing the idea of flames and sparks in a bonfire. This is the stage when children can form a warm bond with one another through sharing in the dance. It is the growth period when imagination can act as a vivid spur to action, enabling mind, feelings, and body to function together.

With regard to imagination, some educators feel that small children should be taught only "concrete" values and that "fantasy" should be kept to a minimum. The author feels that the small child's way of looking at objects and animals is essentially to infuse them with a life of their own, and that imagery derived from this way of seeing things is in keeping with the child's development. "Childhood animism is the tendency to conceive things as living and endowed with intentions. . . . In effect, the small child animates inert bodies and materialises the world of the mind."—Jean Piaget, from his essay "The Mental Development of the Child." Nevertheless, imagery in a class should be used like salt in a stew—to bring out the flavor, but not to overwhelm.

Finally, this is the age of enthusiasm! It is important for adults in charge of children to nurture this most positive quality that all too often gets warped in later life. "Enthusiasm" is derived from the Greek word "enthousia"— meaning "a being possessed by a god"!

•General Comments Pertaining to Skill Levels

SKIPPING

Although most children can gallop at two, they cannot usually skip until they are at least four years old.

HOPPING

Most children cannot hop on one foot at the age of three and a half, but usually learn this skill by four years old. It's important to encourage them to hop equally well on each foot.

MOVING TO A WALTZ RHYTHM

The waltz or 3/4 rhythm (as in WONDERFUL) poses more challenges than the 2/4 rhythm (as in BINGO) or the 4/4 rhythm (as in ELEVATOR). At this stage the ability to speak and clap to a waltz rhythm, with the accent on the first beat, can be gradually acquired. The ability to move round the room keeping time to the waltz beat with the feet, can be acquired by a few if *the first beat only* is used for a jump, stamp, or body swing (as in Jump 2 3, Jump 2 3). The skill to move a foot on each of the three beats, while accenting the first beat, is too difficult for this stage—it means that the first beat of each bar would be accented first on one foot, then on the other, and would require a sophisticated shift in body weight. Even many adults find waltzing difficult! If *no* accent is given to the first beat of each bar, a child may be able to move a foot on each beat, but this is really just a continuous movement as in walking or running, and the character of the waltz is then lost. For the above reasons it is usually best to avoid using waltzes to accompany this age group. An exception could be the use of a slow, dreamy waltz as background music for drifting, expanding, or other slow continuous movement.

•Circle Activities

The circle is again an excellent formation from which to start. While making the acquaintance of both teacher and the other boys and girls, children can begin the dancing class in a safe space.

If you find you are largely working with older three year olds circle activities in the last chapter will still be useful. The fact that children are attending with little adult support is in itself an advance. Below are progressions of some of these activities plus some completely new things to do.

As in the preceding chapter, circle activities not only provide useful ways of beginning and ending a class, but are also valuable tools for refocusing attention in the middle of a class. Something which is learnt in the circle may sometimes be followed up at once by the children creating their own variations and acting them out all around the room.

Rhythm Activities

GENERAL MOVEMENTS

It's helpful to begin with the simple clapping, tapping, and shaking routine used for the previous age group (see "Rhythm Activities" in Chapter Six). Gradually, however, shoulders, chests, tummies, knees, hips, backs, etc., can also express the rhythm as they move back and forth, side to side, round and round, or up and down. Sitting, kneeling, standing, or even lying, may be useful base positions. Shoulder shrugs, knee bounces, arm circles, hip wiggles, head flops, elbow thrusts, etc. are all suitable movements for accenting the rhythm. The resultant movements are, as may be expected, frequently found in primitive dance rituals.

QUALITY OF MOVEMENTS

As well as merely "keeping the beat," movements of a specific character may be introduced, e.g., gentle rocking; assertive punching or kicking movements; floating arm swings; sharp thrusts with different parts of the body; small wriggling movements, etc. After a while children often find themselves enjoying a type of movement they may not have easily found for themselves because it would have been "out of character" for them.

VOCALIZING, AS AN AID TO RHYTHM

In the previous chapter, a single repeated sound such as a tambourine beat or the words "Jump, jump, jump" accompanied by clapping, speaking, and moving. Now more complex rhythm patterns may be used. It's often easier for children to speak to a rhythm pattern than to move to it. For this reason, when they speak a rhythm it helps their bodies to co-ordinate with it. To do this, each syllable requires a clap, shake, nod, or similar movement. Take the rhythms slowly at first, and repeat several times.

Vocal patterns can consist of word phrases or nonsense sounds. Examples of *nonsense sounds* are, WICKY WAM; DUMPY DUMPY DOO DA; YUMPITY YUM. Examples of suitable word phrases are, CHOCOLATE CHIP; GO GO GO AWAY; PLEASE COME BACK; VERY SLEEPY. Combined nonsense and word phrases are often successful, such as, YUM PUM PUM—HERE'S MY DRUM; DIDDLEDY DEE, GIVE IT TO ME; TIC TOC GOES MY CLOCK. Many nursery rhymes make use of these combinations, such as DIDDLE DIDDLE DUMPLING MY SON JOHN; LITTLE TOMMY TITTLE MOUSE LIVED IN A LITTLE HOUSE.

The names of the children in the class can provide good rhythm *material; so can the names of animals. It's helpful to bring along some small toy animals whose names have one, two, and three syllables, for example, FROG, RABBIT, and LADY BUG. Putting these toys in the middle of the circle and pointing at each one in turn provides a basis for the children to clap and speak in rhythm patterns. For example, one might try FROG FROG FROG RABBIT; or LADYBUG LADYBUG FROG RABBIT.*

MAKING A CAKE (A VOCALIZED RHYTHM GAME)

Let's make a cake! What goes into a cake! (Very often an improbable list will follow! This is not an ordinary cake—the children won't mind if there are fifteen eggs, a pot of jam, peanut butter, strawberries, and potato chips in it!)

Let's pretend the middle of the circle is a big bowl. We'll start with the eggs. Let's break them like this: CRACK-SPLOSH! CRACK-SPLOSH! CRACK-SPLOSH! etc. Now let's stir them up. STIR STIR STIR STIR STIR STIR STIR, etc. Now for the pot of jam. Let's shake the jam out of the pot—GLUG GLUG GLUG GLUG GLUG GLUG—G-DOING! . . . into the bowl it goes! Let's pretend that we're *the jam being shaken out in big shakes—here we go! Now we'll stir* that *up. STIR STIR etc.*

Let's crumble the potato chips in one by one now—SCRUMPH SCRUMPH SCRUMPH SCRUMPH SCRUMPH SCRUMPH. What about adding some milk to all these things? We'll pour it from a jug. PLOPPITY PLOP, PLOPPITY PLOP, PLOPPITY PLOP. Now we'll go Ploppity plop, flopping about in the bowl here as if we had no bones and were all runny and floppy and ploppy like the milk.

Other ingredients	*Suggested Sounds*	*Suggested Actions*
Sugar	Shhhhhh!	Trembling shake, first with hands, then with whole body.
Strawberries	Click with tongue	Light flick with fingers then light wide hop from one foot to the other.

Peanut Butter	Oogy Googy	Brushing one hand across the other with resistance, then dragging one foot then the other.
Flour	Foooooo!	Lightly floating falling hands, then same movement with whole body.

Many other ingredients will be thought of. There is no literal attempt to translate the hand mime into the body movement. Rather, the aim is to enhance a feeling for the quality of the movement.

When the cake has been stirred for the last time it can be carried to the oven where it rises. Everyone can rise slowly like the cake. Then the cake can be taken out and left to cool (an exercise in stillness and silence for a few seconds). It may then be iced with a wide, spreading motion—SHOOOOOOOOO WOOOOOOOOO SHOOOOOOOOO WOOOOOOOOO. Candles can be stuck in the top (children can jump "on" one by one and be "lit"). The flames can flicker, the candle can shrink, and then be blown out. The cake can be cut—K, K, K, K, K, K, (large slicing action with arms) and finally—eaten!

What differentiates a game of this type from a drama game are the repetitive rhythms invoked by voice and body, giving the movements a dance quality. Other games of this kind, in which there is rhythmic integration of voice and movement in a fun scenario, can easily be invented. Two suggestions are: Washing the Clothes, and Gardening in the Vegetable Patch.

PERCUSSION

Accompanying music with simple percussion instruments which can be tapped or shaken can be a more refined alternative to the rattle boxes described in the previous chapter. Tambourines, rhythm sticks, rhythm blocks, jingle bells, are all useful. A strong loud lead from teacher and/or accompanist will be required to maintain the beat.

Locating Different Parts of the Body

Between two and a half and three and a half, the task of locating the correct part of the body and touching it when named, occupied most of the attention. Between three and a half and four and a half, this procedure can be turned into a coordination and speed game. It can be developed further by setting more difficult problems:

Can you touch your shoulders? Change hands!

Put one hand on your tummy and one on your back. Now change hands as quickly as you can. Change, change, change!

Now put one hand on your knee and one hand on your head. Change!

Can you put your head and one knee on the floor at the same time?

Can you touch your back on the floor while your feet are in the air?

Can you put one shoulder and the other hand on the floor?

Can you touch somebody else's hand? (Some children do not like touching anyone else at first. In this case it's best to leave them to themselves until they are ready to join in.)

As a follow up activity let the children do a "back," "shoulder," "head," dance, etc., as they move all round the room with special emphasis on moving the chosen part.

An imaginative way of achieving the same result is to play "Paint Pot." This game was introduced to me at a Joyce Boorman dance workshop for teachers of dance to children in Grades 1, 2, and 3.

PAINT POT

Let's pretend we have a big pot full of red paint. We'll put our heads in it and get our hair all covered with sticky red paint. Now let's flop that paint off our heads all over the place ...... FLOP, FLOP, FLOP! What part shall we put in now? All right, let's put our foot in. Now we'll go STAMP STAMP STAMP with that foot all over the floor and pretend we're making big red splodges. (This idea can be extended to many parts of the body and to many types of movement.)

Now let's pretend that we have another pot all full of blue paint.

We'll get into the pot right up to our necks! Now we'll climb out again all blue! How can we get this sticky blue paint all over the room? That's right, let's shake ourselves like doggies! Now how can we make the floor all blue? Yes, we can bounce up and down like this! That's another good idea—we'll roll over and over and over all over the floor.

At this point in the game a child may say, "Let's pour the paint on the floor!", or "Let's kick the paint pot over!", which is fine, as the suggestions then become part of the dance.

Training Speed of Response

"HOT"—A CIRCLE GAME

Let's kneel down in the circle. The piano (tambourine, drum, etc.) is going to say CRASH—like this! Now we'll slowly reach one hand forward in the air and when we hear the loud crash we'll pretend that we've touched something hot and bring it back quickly like this. (The first time around the children are slow to respond.) *Now let's do it again.* (Repeat several times.) *Let's do it with the other hand. How about doing it with both hands? Can you do it with your foot? That's harder isn't it? How about the other foot? Let's try and do it with our heads now . . . . . . We'll bend forward slowly, like this, and when we hear the CRASH, up will come our heads! Now this time when we bring our heads up quickly we'll say HI to everybody!*

Singing Activities

Once more, this is a good way to finish a class. The songs suggested in the previous chapter may be supplemented by others, some of which have greater intervals between the notes. Popular ones are:

Mary had a little lamb
The Muffin Man
Jingle Bells (in season!)
Inky Winky Spider
Frère Jacques or Are you Sleeping?

Hot

Some of the qualities expressed through dancing may also be expressed through singing. For example:

Singing a song very quietly and lightly

Starting a song very quietly and gradually getting louder and louder (corresponds to getting heavier)

Starting a song very loudly and gradually getting quieter and slower, etc.

These techniques tend to eliminate the out of tune shouting which is the way three and four years olds often sing when they haven't been guided to listen to the music.

Our Own Dance in the Circle

Dancing one by one in the circle, as before, is very popular. If a child is reluctant to have a turn at first, he may enjoy dancing with a partner. Again, the rule is not to pressure. Interestingly enough, a child who is slow to join in other activities may get off the ground through doing a solo in the circle, and receiving the spotlight of concentrated attention.

Whereas with the younger group it was merely enough for the child to jump or run on the spot, now the circle dance serves many functions:

DIVERSITY

Diversity is encouraged when children watch and want to imitate new dances which others are doing, and, in turn, become inspired to find a new way of dancing themselves. When a child has learned a new way of moving (such as hopping or skipping) he will quite rightly wish to repeat it many times. Repetition which comes from joy of achievement, and repetition which comes from being unwilling to venture forth, should be differentiated. The former is characterized by general enthusiasm, the latter by apathy.

Children at this stage may not be content to be just repetitive for the 20 seconds or so of the dance, but may prefer to give two or three movement variations. For example, they could give a hop on one foot, followed by spinning, followed by a dance on the tummy. This tendency should be encouraged.

Own dance

Most children under four years old want the music to start before they "make up a dance." In effect, they need a stimulus to get them going, although after a few seconds they may quite happily settle into their own rhythm and tempo—versatile accompanying is therefore desirable. Somewhere around four years old, children can start their own dance without the aid of music or percussion. In this case the rhythmic accompaniment will, from the start, follow the rhythm initiated by the child.

MONITORING

Monitoring of movements is easier when dealing with children one by one as they dance in the circle. Tendencies to turn always in the same direction, to dance always on the toes, to thump consistently with the feet, to use the torso and arms rarely, to dance usually at the same tempo, etc., can be counteracted by suggesting a contrasting dance after the child's own choice.

GENERAL OBSERVATION OF POSTURE

This is a good time to become aware of obvious posture faults such as flat feet, sway back, slumped shoulders, etc. This book does not offer specific remedial exercises. Parents should gently be informed of observed posture faults, and a suggestion should be made that it would be desirable to have the condition medically checked out and remedial exercises begun. When the child is still small these faults can often be remedied easily, whereas when growth has stopped correction is usually far more difficult to achieve.

There are several reasons for bad posture, *one* of which is emotional. The psycho-physical exercise of progressively freeing the body through dance, often counteracts emotional causes of bad posture. This fact can be observed if one works with a child with "problems" over a number of years. For example, a child who generally hangs his head and contracts his chest, and is also very shy, may little by little come to hold his spine more erect when he gains confidence in movement.

Again, possible hearing problems may be discovered in a child who never seems to hear the beat of the music when dancing by himself—though poor coordination may also be responsible.

Using the Space of the Whole Room, including On the Floor Dances

The starter activities described under these headings in the previous chapter are useful to get this age group going also. After a week or two, however, when children have settled in and have danced with a variety of movements, a very popular game may be introduced:

THE MAGIC DANCE

This game is called "The Magic Dance." We can do it either standing up or moving down on the floor. Now will one of you show us a dance so that we can all do it too? Thank you, Erica. (Erica gives about 5 seconds of a repetitive movement, travelling across the floor, around in a circle or on the spot.) *That's an interesting dance—let's all do Erica's dance now.* (About 20 seconds is enough.) *Now who can show us a* different *dance?* Go head, Peter. (etc.)

In this way most of the children are likely to contribute a movement. This improves their self-confidence. They also learn to observe from an assortment of leaders, and increase their vocabulary of movement thereby.

UNACCOMPANIED CREATIVE DANCE AROUND THE ROOM

Towards the end of the year when most of the children have become self- starters, suggest that they do their own dance around the room all at the same time with no musical accompaniment. Suggest that they do whatever dance they first think of without copying anyone else, and that they come and sit down beside you when they have danced for long enough.

Children may then do fine, rhythmical dances for several minutes. Some like to keep repeating the same action—others will change the pattern every twenty seconds or so. As there is now no external stimulus to motivate the children, what they do will be based on the satisfaction they derive from whatever movements they choose. Sometimes they come and sit down for half a minute, then get up and dance again. This can quite happily continue for several minutes. In a little while everyone stays sitting down. At this point they usually look both contented and a little tired.

ANIMALS

Mimicking animal motion is again useful for movement exploration around the room. It's now possible to ask the class to show how a rabbit, spider, butterfly, etc., move, without first demonstrating. Memory can serve as the basis from which to copy. However, there is quite often a wide discrepancy between what a child *thinks* he is conveying and what in fact, he conveys. Therefore, a dog, a lion, and a bear might all be depicted in the same way, and guidance would be needed in characterizing further. A game in which each child chooses an animal to demonstrate to the rest who then "guess" what it is, helps children to understand how much they are communicating (or not communicating) in movement. On one occasion a four year old boy gave a splendid display of crouching, running, widely flapping his arms, and hoarsely shrieking! "Now what's *that*?" he said, turning round and challenging me.

"A duck? ... A seagull?"

"No," he said triumphantly, "a pteradactyl!"

•Sensory Contrasts and Sensory Combinations

The entire section on sensory contrasts and combinations in the previous chapter can be used, with judicious selection, for this stage as well. That section dealt with contrasts under the headings of Tempo (fast or slow); Weight (light or heavy); Size, and Contracting and Expanding (big or small and out or in); Degree of Tension (floppy or stiff) and Levels (high or low). More examples of things to do in the above categories follow:

Tempo

Children have now reached the stage when they can give more definition to miming the movement of different creatures through varying their impressions of speed and weight. A guided exercise encouraging this will therefore complement the preceding "guessing" game. The following are examples of speed variations: a horse galloping; a tortoise shuffling; a bird swooping; a snail creeping; a fish darting; a cat prowling.

The following is a movement game in which the children follow the accompaniment in order to produce varying tempos:

THE MIXED UP MACHINE

Do you know how a machine moves? Yes, it's usually stiff and jerky—let's make up a stiff and jerky movement that we keep doing again and again the way a machine does. (Through guided discovery a variety of ways of moving like a machine will emerge.) *Now you choose one of those movements, and the piano (percussion, guitar, etc.) will make the machine sound for you . . . . . . like this. Now we'll pretend that your machine gets mixed up; it doesn't know what speed to go and it keeps stopping and starting. Listen to the music and make your machine do what the music does.* Many variations of speed can now be given. Sometimes give a long pause, sometimes a short one, before a new speed is taken up. Sometimes let the tempo change gradually, sometimes all at once. The rhythm can also be varied—for example, *CHA* CHA could be changed to DIDDLE *DUM* or BONKITY *BOO!*)

Weight

Examples of heavily and lightly moving creatures are: an elephant treading; a crocodile dragging; a whale rolling; a butterfly fluttering; a mouse scampering; a bird lightly landing.

Examples of light and heavy nature objects also provide suitable material: clouds floating; snowflakes drifting; raindrops pattering; heavy branches swaying; big rocks rolling, etc.

The following story illustrates light, medium and heavy weight movements, expressed in a variety of directions:

THE GRANDFATHER CLOCK

Once there was a big, brown Grandfather Clock. Lots of little seconds lived inside it. They spoke to themselves very quietly like this: TICK TICK TICK TICK (light jumping on the spot). *Lots of minutes lived inside it too. They spoke a little louder like this, TICK-TOCK TICK-TOCK TICK-TOCK TICK-TOCK* (medium weight rocking on the spot from foot to foot). *And then there were twelve hours which lived in there. And each hour made a big booming sound every now and then like this—BOOM!* (Standing with feet apart and heavily swinging clasped hands through legs and up again.) *If it was three o'clock there were three booms. If it was five o'clock there were five.*

Well the Grandfather Clock was not happy. All the minutes and hours had been having a fight and they sounded like this: (Random mixture of several BOOMS and several TIC-TOCKS). *"I can't stand this," said the Grandfather Clock," it's messing up my machinery. I'm going to stop!" And it did.*

Then all the little seconds and minutes and hours tumbled out of the door in the front of the Grandfather Clock, and started to wander round the room, forgetting their quarrel for a while.

"It's a very big world out here," said the seconds, jumping lightly all about—from side to side, backwards and forwards, round and round, and feeling lost and frightened, trying to fill up all the space.

"It's a very cold world out here," said the minutes, rocking not too lightly, not too heavily—all about, from side to side, backwards and forwards, round and round, and in all different ways, like this (on knees from side to side), *and this* (sitting down, back and forth), *and this* (on back, rolling from side to side), *etc., trying to keep warm.*

"It's a very quiet world out here," said the hours booming all over the kitchen in all directions, like this (swiping up in the air like a golf club) *and this* (swinging around the head like a hammer), *and this* (whacking the air from side to side in front like a broom), *trying to fill up the silence of the room.*

But it was no good. The seconds and minutes and hours did not like it out there, in the big, cold, quiet room. So they climbed quietly back in through the door in the front of the Grandfather Clock.

"Had enough?" asked the big, brown Grandfather Clock.

"TICK TICK TICK TICK," said the seconds in a proper way again (lightly jumping on the spot).

"TICK-TOCK TICK-TOCK TICK-TOCK TICK-TOCK," said the minutes in a proper way again (medium weight rocking from side to side and from foot to foot on the spot).

And at one o'clock and not before there was one very proper "BOOM!"

"That's better," said the Grandfather Clock. "I don't think my machinery will go wrong again for a long time now." And it didn't!

Size and Contracting and Expanding

At this stage it's still best to maintain a stationary base while becoming familiar with the feeling of growing larger and smaller.

THE TULIP

Once there was a little Tulip bulb in the earth. When the Spring came, a tiny green shoot grew slowly out of it, like this. It pushed its way up through the earth. "What's going to happen to me now?" said the shoot.

At the end of the shoot was a small bud. When the sun came and warmed it, it opened out slowly, like this. "What's going to happen to me now?" said the bud.

Round the bud, deep pink petals began to open slowly in the sun, like this. "What's going to happen to us now?" said the petals.

When the petals got tired of stretching out, they began to droop, like this. Then they just dropped gently off, one by one, in this way. "What's going to happen to me now?" said the stalk once more.

As the stalk got tired of standing up straight, it bent over like this. "What's going to happen to me now?" said the Tulip. Just then the wind swept by and blew the stalk right over onto the earth. Then the wind swept by again.

"You'll be all right, Tulip," said the wind. "Next year you'll grow again when the sun begins to warm you."

All winter long the Tulip bulb lay still in the earth, sleeping and dreaming of the sun. When Spring came, a little green shoot began to grow again, just like the wind said it would. The Tulip was happy to know that it would go on growing again, and again.

Shall we do that dance again?

Contracting and Expanding can also be expressed by miming the movements of a balloon being blown up and let down. A full description of this can be found further on in this section of sensory contrasts, under the heading of Sudden and Sustained Movements.

Degree of Tension in the Body

Here is a poem which helps in developing the feeling of contrast between a tense position and a relaxed "floppy" one:

Tulip bulbs waiting for the spring

THE PUPPET

I'm always danced by someone else,
They stretch and pull and flop me;
Arms, legs, head and back,
Just like an old potato sack,
They lift me up, then drop me!

Limbs, back, neck, all stretch out into extended "stiff" positions, one by one, as if being held and stretched by someone else. Then the positions are suddenly "let go" as if being dropped, one by one, resulting in floppy collapse. Experiment with this theme with as many parts of the body from as many different starting positions as possible. Ask for examples from the children

Well now I have a special plan—
When everyone's asleep,
When all is quiet, I'll take a look,
I'll wriggle off my puppet hook
And fall into a heap.

Pretend puppet is hanging by a tab at the back of its neck with extended back and floppy head position. Wriggling of back causes puppet to "come off the hook" then to collapse. See how many ways of collapsing can be discovered by leading the action with first one, then another part of the body.

I'll try to get up by myself
And see what I can do;
I'll see if I can kick and spin,
Stretch right out and curl right in—
I'll dance as well as you!

Practice getting up, leading with one part of the body at a time. Ask the children to try and get up without any part of them becoming stiff on the way—this results in a flowing action. This verse can, of course, be used to evoke many different ways of moving. Most children are eager to give examples of ways the puppet has found to dance. After the puppet has done a lot of moving and proved its

Puppet arms about to flop down

Floppy puppet heads

autonomy, it lies down, has a rest, and reverts to the helpless puppet state again.

You can now quietly walk around, gently lifting a hand or a foot an inch or two off the floor, then letting them go again. With a very relaxed child, you may try carefully rolling a head from side to side, or gently raising a child's hips an inch off the floor, then releasing them equally gently. The aim is to encourage the child to relax the body completely, and to maintain the degree of relaxation while part of their body is moved, so that it has "floppy weight".

Some children are more tense and less trusting than others and it is quite a breakthrough when they can develop the attitude of yielding rather than using their will to resist or assist. You should handle the children with sensitivity and care. If a child is grabbed too suddenly, or if a hand is let go with too much of a thump, confidence and relaxation are undermined.

After the "letting go" exercise, the puppet can lift itself onto the hook again, so that no one will suspect its adventures.

Although the primary aim of "The Puppet" poem is to develop awareness of tension and relaxation in the body, the idea of "passive" and "active" ways of moving has also been touched on. This latter idea will be further developed in the next chapter.

Levels

In the preceding chapter, children were only consciously encouraged to think of two levels—high and low. Of course they discovered movements at intervening levels without being aware of the concept of level. At this stage it's possible to add a "middle" level which can be found by the children when asked to produce it.

Moving the whole body higher and higher, then lower and lower in stages, helps to develop the feeling for level. Music is a good "coat hanger" for the following activity: the child moves down a level on each note as the rhyme is sung to a descending scale.

Down, down, down, down,
Leaves are falling, gold and brown.

This one can be used to reverse the process, while sung to an ascending scale:

Up, up, up the tree,
Up I'm climbing—look at me!

THE BEAR AND THE HONEY

This game, involving pitch of sound and level of position, can be played as before in the previous chapter. But now a middle position can be added corresponding to a middle note (Middle C would be appropriate). We now have:

A low note — Bear crouched at bottom of tree
A middle note — Bear half standing up, front paws off ground but back and knees bent
A high note — Bear reaching for honey high in the tree.

These notes are played at random and the children must find the corresponding positions. Before adding the middle note you should make sure that the children can readily differentiate between high and low, without giving them a lead. When they become fairly proficient at the game with three levels, ask them to try it with their eyes closed, so they cannot copy one another.

The following is a useful poem for evoking movement at different levels, particularly in the middle range (less stretched up than normal human posture).

MINGUS THE MONKEY

Mingus the Monkey just sits when he's sunning,
But Mingus the Monkey is clever at running—
He raises his front feet a bit off the ground
And he's off through the trees with a charge and a bound!

Mingus the Monkey curls up when he's sleeping,
But Mingus the Monkey is clever at leaping—
He hangs from his fingers and swings all the rest
Then he lands on his feet and he puffs out his chest!

Mingus the Monkey, he doesn't take chances,
He's very sure-footed when moving on branches—
He runs on all four of his long fingered feet
Then he hangs upside down to cool off in the heat!

Oh I do wish that I was so clever and spunky
And able to clamber as Mingus the Monkey!

Further sensory contrasts:

In addition to the foregoing contrasts, three rather more subtle contrasts can be explored at this point. These three contrasts are not entirely new, for children in the preceding age group will have begun to experience them—however it is now possible to work on them more deliberately: sudden and sustained movements; abandoned and controlled movements; movement itself and stillness.

Sudden and Sustained Movements

(A sustained movement may be a flowing movement or a prolonged continuous movement.)

When most small children do sudden movements they are usually neither particularly light nor particularly heavy because of their limited control and strength. They can manage light, sustained, flowing movements, however, such as smoke drifting and leaves falling; and they can manage a heavy, sustained movement, such as an airplane dipping and turning.

Although they do not easily understand the concept behind this contrast, they understand the feeling within the movement. It is best, therefore, to give examples in imagery and weave them into stories, games, and other activities.

Here are three dance games which contain quite a number of sudden movements, and quite a number of sustained movements.

MIST, LIGHTNING, WHIRLWIND
(This is also a good listening and remembering activity)

Weather Word	Suggested Sound	Suggested Movement
MIST (Sustained)	Instrumental music—slow, flowing, dreamy; or rising and falling humming sound in which children join in.	Slow, locomotor floor movement—rolling, dragging slowly, slow motion creeping, etc.

LIGHTNING (Sudden)	Trill on piano or shake on tambourine	Sharp, incisive jumps and arm shakes which start and stop suddenly with the accompaniment
WHIRLWIND (Sustained)	Arpeggios on piano or sustained roll on gong or cymbal in which sound increases and decreases in volume, but keep on going	Flowing, spinning motion from various positions

First, the children are familiarized with the weather word and its related musical sound. Explorations in movement then follow for each one. The weather word is then dropped and only the music is played for each one, in random order. When the children get mixed up, they are reminded of the weather word again.

THE BALLOON

How does a balloon look before it is blown up? That's right, all flat and squished. Now let's pretend that we're the balloon and that someone is going to blow us up in one slow blow.... Shhhhhhhhhhhhhhhhh! We grow bigger and fatter and fatter and bigger until we're all round and light. Now we go gently floating up and down, up and down, up and down, all over the place.

But the person who blew us up didn't tie us up well enough. The air is slowly coming out and we get more and more thin and droopy, until we just go Aaaaaaaaaaaaaa! And we're all squished again.

This time the person blows us up in lots of quick short blows and we suddenly GROW. . . . and GROW. . . . and GROW and then the person just lets go of us and we go shooting about all over the room like this in one long whizz! Zzzzzzzzzzzzzzzzzzzzz!

Now we're going to be blown up slowly again..Shhhhhhhhhh! But the person forgets to stop blowing—we're so big we're going to go POP! Wait for the sound (Percussion, piano, voice, etc.) POP! We jump into a heap very quickly. Let's do that again. Shhhhhhhhhhhhhhhh! . . . . . . Are you ready? POP!

Well now, let's pretend that we're slowly drawing a balloon in the air in front of us with our finger, in a big, slow circle. (Each hand separately and then both hands together.) *What color is your balloon?* (Asking specific questions about the image helps children to visualize what they are doing.) *Now let's turn around and draw another balloon in another color, and another and another, etc. Now the room is full of big balloons that you've all drawn in the air.*

Let's pretend now that there's a big pin-cushion here full of sharp, shiny pins. We're going to pull one out with each hand and then go jumping around in all directions pricking the balloons sharply, and quickly, and making them POP like this . . . . *POP!..POP!..POP!..POP!*

THE TREE

(This is also an exercise in expanding, up to the time the tree is chopped down)

The children do the action along with you as you speak . . .

Once I was a tree. First of all I was a little seed in the ground and then I grew and grew and grew. My roots got stronger and longer under the earth. (Lying curled on the ground and slowly reaching limbs out in all directions.) *My trunk grew up and up.* (Curled position again, and slowly rising with palms together, above head.) *My branches spread out like this.* (Slowly extend arms outwards. Bring them back and extend them again several times, each time stretching them in different directions. Then try growing branches with alternate arms.) *Little leaves grew out of the ends of my branches.* (Hands 'quiver' all around.) *Then along came the wind.* (The branches sway, as the whole body, anchored on spread apart feet, slowly and heavily sways around.)

One day a man came along to chop me down. He had a big axe and chopped me like this! (Powerful chopping motion.) *Now let's change hands and chop from the other side.*

After a while, I just toppled over. (Slow fall ending with drop onto ground. Children shouldn't fall in a straight line as a tree does or they will jar their backs and bang their heads. Instead they should crumple up—knee, hip, side, shoulder and lastly, head.)

Then I was made into a nice, strong picnic table. Perhaps you have seen me in a campsite?

Abandoned and Controlled Movements

This contrast is particularly useful for children who tend to be either too inhibited or too overactive. While stories, poems, and music can evoke these qualities, the following dance and movement games are specially designed to bring out the contrast between abandoned and controlled movement.

MARY MARY QUITE CONTRARY

Everyone gallops or skips in a very "proper" and controlled way as they intone the words "Mary Mary" to suitable gentle accompaniment or tambourine beat. Then after a brief pause there is a crash on the drum (tambourine, gong,) a sudden change of mood, and everyone cavorts wildly round while yelling loudly, "Quite Contrary," to clashing, discordant accompaniment, if available. The wild part of the dance can consist of banging the floor, abandoned rolling, rocking, hammering feet on the floor, arms wildly flailing back and forth, generally shaking the body and leaping, etc. The children enjoy finding as many wild ways of moving as they can.

THE PARCEL

Bring two parcels to class. Unwrap the first one very carefully and then do it up again with equal precision and care (holding it together with scotch tape). The children then pretend that they are the parcel being carefully unwrapped: from a bunched up position on their backs they carefully "unwrap" each arm and leg until they are lying flat like a smooth piece of paper. Then just as deliberately, they wrap up their limbs again.

Now demonstrate the unwrapping of the second parcel. Grab at the paper and hurriedly pull it off into a crumpled heap. After flattening out the paper in a swift stroke, quickly squish it back on again in an irregular fashion with bits left sticking up in the air. The children now "unwrap" themselves in an abandoned manner, twisting themselves into different shapes as they do so. Then after momentarily and suddenly flattening out, they quickly wriggle up their arms and legs into a scrambled heap!

HUMPTY DUMPTY

Gently rock to and fro with the children, like Humpty Dumpty sitting on the wall. The rocking action becomes larger, so that eventually Humpty Dumpty tips off—collapses and sprawls. This can be done from sitting, kneeling, and standing positions. The "fall" is an exercise in abandoned collapse into random positions. Despite the degree of "letting go" advise the children to let their heads down last to avoid bumping them (they usually do this naturally).

The following poem may be used to illustrate light movements which are both contained and slow, and abandoned and fast.

TWO SNOWFLAKES
I see a snowflake slowly fall,
It turns and makes no sound at all.
Gently, gently twisting round
It comes to rest upon the ground.

Another one is spinning by,
This one seems to whirl and fly;
Faster, faster round it goes
Before it settles on my nose!

ALARM CLOCK

(In this activity a gentle, contained walk changes suddenly to abandoned leaping.)

Have you ever seen an alarm clock? Well this is an alarm clock. Can you hear it saying TCHK TCHK TCHK TCHK TCHK? Now I'm going to set the alarm clock for a minute or two from now. There—it will make a loud buzzing sound in a little while. Let's just step gently from foot to foot, lifting our knees high and going for a little walk around the room while the clock goes TCHK TCHK TCHK TCHK and I make this noise on the tambourine at the same time. Now, when it buzzes, let's jump in the air and wave our arms and hands and heads all over the place. Are you ready for the buzz to come in a minute? Keep stepping from foot to foot—remember to lift your knees high—any second now—BZZZZZZZZZZZZZZZZ-ZZZZZZZZ! . . . . . . It's slowing down . . . Z-Z-Z-Z-Z-Z! It's stopped. Have you stopped?

Retiring children naturally find it hard to move in an abandoned way. Though they hang back at first they frequently come to enjoy the sensation of impulsive freedom in movement, even if it takes them a while to acquire it. By contrast, highly active extrovert children will almost at once enjoy moving in a "careful" way as long as it is part of a fun sequence, and as long as it is for a short time only. They will start being "silly" with the movement if they have to do it for too long. It is nevertheless a good idea to prolong, bit by bit, the intervals of time in which they have to move in a restrained and careful way, as it helps them to calm down momentarily.

Motion and Stillness

When one thinks of dance one automatically envisages movement. However, it is the slight suspensions between movements and the occasional pauses that help to give the dance definition. In fact the patterns of stillness between movements are an integral part of dancing.

In professional dancing it is the choreographer who charts the movement-pause pattern which others then follow. In creative dance, one must learn to create it for oneself—although a small child can only come to terms with the more obvious aspects of motion and stillness.

Often a movement depends on a particular kind of brief, initial pause. For example, a spring or leap requires a preceding pause in a contracted position of contained energy (observe a cat drawing back and pausing before a spring). Swinging movements depend on a slight suspension between them when the impetus has run out in one direction, and before the body weight carries the swing back in the opposite direction. A spin requires a curled up instant preceding it, twisting in the opposite direction to that which the motion will take. This kind of initial pause is linked to the correct preparation of body weight. Small children should develop a sensory appreciation of this still moment of preparation, through observation and practice, rather than an intellectual one.

There is a pause before the beginning and after the end of the dance for which children should develop awareness. It is not desirable for children to get into the habit of haphazard beginnings and endings which lack sensitivity and control. The music can provide a very good objective timing device. Before beginning it is useful to say, "Are you ready?" and to stop any false starts (as in a running race). When everyone is still and listening there is a type of anticipation out of which much more concentrated and meaningful movement can flow. At the end of the dance, the music can begin to slow down a little and again it is helpful to say, "Slow down gently, we're going to stop!" Some children are simply not used to listening very much and it will take them a while to catch on, but it is never too soon to encourage this kind of listening response, to help it become a habit.

Another type of stillness may occur when dancing with a partner or a group. Not all the children will necessarily move all the time, particularly if they are enacting different characters. The ability to keep still in a chosen position and to stay *within* the dance rather than to drop out physically and psychically, is an art which is gradually acquired. It is like learning to listen in a conversation rather than wanting to speak all the time. Its practice may be begun at this age but by no means mastered. This skill may best be encouraged through invoking the imagination rather than through giving a meaningless physical order not to move. For example, "This little mouse under the leaves keeps very still as the bear creeps by," will be far more effective than "Don't move when Steven is passing you!"

For the most part, children in this age group still tend to move in a continuous repetitive way (as in a primitive dance) even though the movements themselves change from time to time on a random basis. Pauses within the dance are therefore rarely thought of unless they are there for some reason (dramatic, verbal, musical, etc.).

The following are activities to develop sensitivity for moments of stillness in dancing—

THE CAMERA GAME

Let's grow into a curled up shape—now stay still a minute as I'm going to pretend to take a photograph of you—CLICK! Can you move a little bit now still staying almost in that shape?

Let's grow into a stretched out shape—stay quite still, here comes another photograph—CLICK! Now let's see if you can move about in that shape.

Now let's grow all droopy and just hang over like this. Stay still for the camera again—CLICK! Can we move in a droopy way now?

Let's see if we can grow all stiff and prickly looking like a cactus.

...any shape we like

Now see if you can stay extra still because I'm going to take two photographs this time—CLICK! CLICK! I wonder if we can move in a stiff, prickly way?

This time let's get into any shape we like. Put your arms and legs and back and head into some interesting shape—quite different from everyone else's shape. Now hold still . . . . . . be very careful not to move now, because this time I'm going to walk in and out of you taking lots of photographs. CLICK!...CLICK!...CLICK!...CLICK!... CLICK! That's very good.

Now let's jump up and down and shake ourselves a lot!

STATUES IN THE PARK

Once there was a park with a lot of statues in it. Do you know what a statue is? It's like a picture made out of stone. You can walk around it. These statues were made in the shape of people—all in different positions. But they were always still because they were made of stone. Now let's grow into the shape of the statues . . . . . . and now let's stay quite still.

Now once upon a time a magic moonbeam got into the park. When it shone on the statues they started to move, one by one. It came up to each of them like this...(With bell, triangle, or finger cymbal make a "TING" sound near a child's ear.) *Now when the moonbeam talks to you like that, you find that you can move slowly, round and round in the air and over the ground.*

Are you ready for the moonbeam to talk to you? Off we go. ("TING" near each child in turn until all the children are moving . . . at first they may have difficulty learning to move one at a time because the copying instinct is strong. With a little practice, most of them can manage it, however.)

Now you're all turning slowly about the park in the moonlight. But here comes the gardener! He has forgotten his coat and has come back for it. You can hear him coming because I'm going to make a thumping on the drum as he walks towards you. (Thump on drum or tambourine.) *Now when I give a big bang he stops in surprise . . . . . . and you must all stop too and grow quickly back into your statue shapes again. THUMP THUMP THUMP THUMP THUMP THUMP BANG! Don't move! Are you all quite still? Stay where you are in your statue shape again. Now let's try that again ... Here comes the gardener ... THUMP THUMP THUMP THUMP THUMP THUMP* BANG! *Grow quickly into your statue shape AND STAY QUITE STILL!*

"That's funny," says the gardener, rubbing his eyes. "I thought I saw these statues moving. Oh dear, maybe I'm having a dream!" And off he goes without his coat, shaking his head. THUMP THUMP THUMP THUMP THUMP THUMP THUMP....and he's gone!

Now the children are familiar with the idea of this game, repeat it. Encourage them to grow into a different shape this time, and speak as little as you need to.

REPEAT OF THE STORY OF "THE SPIDER AND THE FLY"
(See the section "More Stories, Poems, and Games," near the end of Chapter Six)

This story can be used again in the following way. Half the children can play the part of spiders and half, the flies. It will probably be hard at first for the younger ones to grasp the idea of maintaining their roles, and to keep still while others are moving. Eventually, however, they learn how to do this. If the children are still attentive, they can swap roles.

LYING QUIETLY—AN EXERCISE IN STILLNESS ONLY

Let's all lie down and not move at all. Here is some very quiet sleepy music. We'll get nice and comfortable. I'll pretend I'm a big bear creeping around and that I can't see you when you're quite still. Oh—I can see Mary's hands moving. A lot of you are making your eyes go all tight and blinking them lots of times. Just close them—let them go droopy inside. Peter's wriggling his feet. Jane's rocking from side to side. Let's pretend that you're a very still stone sinking through the water now. That's right .... O.K. Now I'll pretend I can see you all again. I'll walk in between you and if you are quite still, I'll gently touch your shoulder to let you know you've managed not to move at all...just let's listen to the music and keep quite still.

Because children are very suggestible and you want them to be alert for the rest of the class, it's advisable to say something like this, after the exercise:

Spinning webs

Lying quietly

Let's all wake up now and stretch in big, big stretches! Now we'll all do a wide-awake jumping dance!

Sensory Combinations

As well as the sensory combinations contained in the preceding chapter, one has only to consider familiar daily activities and common objects surrounding one, to realize that they provide good movement material under this heading.

A few examples are:

Digging in the garden — slow and heavy

Pushing a car which is "stuck" — slow and heavy

Falling down the stairs — fast and abandoned

A flag flapping in the breeze — floppy, slow, and light

A flag being held out straight by the wind — stiff, light, and expanded

Water, slowly filling up a bath tub — low to high level, light, and slow

Apple, falling off tree and rolling over the ground — abandoned, curled, and fast

Star, twinkling — fast and light

Long drape, moving in breeze — floppy and fairly heavy

Etc.

•Patterns in Space

Children between three and a half and four and a half have a much better appreciation of space than children a year younger. They are beginning to come to terms with direction (forwards, backwards, sideways, upwards, and downwards, etc.); they are able to "grow" into different shapes and move in an appropriate way to the shapes. They can begin to learn to spread out into the room and find a working space that is not on top of everybody else, and they can discover how to work in a little space or a big space of their own making.

All this means that dancing is beginning to develop a form; random use of space is gradually supplanted by premeditated use of space, or at least by the sense of making up a pattern of some type as one is going along.

Body Shape

Experiment with the same body shapes as in the last chapter, i.e., curled, stretched, humped, flattened, twisted, straightened, etc. But at this age there are more ways of approaching shape making:

CONSECUTIVE SHAPES

There are many pictures or images which may be used to evoke two consecutive shapes such as curling and stretching. For example, a caterpillar calls to mind the idea of humping and flattening out again. A balloon suggests the idea of lying flat and then becoming big and round. A seed growing out of the earth into a tall flower is a good image for curling and stretching tall. Remember to bring objects and pictures to be portrayed, with you to the class.

The following are a few ways of giving tangible or visible examples of shapes to be made by the body.

DRAWING AND DOING

Essentially, this exercise creates a shape on paper which is then translated into a still shape or a "moving shape" with different parts of the body. When children draw shapes on paper first, it seems to clarify their thinking very substantially, and generally leads to their offering interesting and inventive movement examples.

Hand out a piece of paper and a wax crayon to each child. Tell the children not to draw until the special drawing music starts and that you are all going to dance what you have drawn.

Now let's draw dots all over the paper like little drops of rain. Here comes the dot music (staccato accompaniment) DOT DOT DOT DOT DOT DOT DOT! (It's useful to say "Dot" each time you make one. Children will automatically keep in time with the music and the speaking, and thus this exercise also assists the sense of rhythm.) *Now let's put down our crayons and stand up. Can you make dots like that in the air with your fingers?* (Index fingers stab the air all around.) *How would you make dots with your head?* (Heads start nodding all around in the air.) *How would you make dots with your elbows?* (Knees, feet, seat, tummy, etc. Encourage the children to make dots both in the air and on the floor.)

Now let's pick up our crayons again and draw a straight line just like this—to a straight line sound. (A prolonged note on an instrument or a quick "run" up or down the scale would do.) *Now let's draw another, and another, and another. You can make your lines all go across each other if you like. Put your crayons down again, and now let's make our whole self into a straight line. Can you do that any other way?* (Both lying down and standing up shapes are usually offered.) *Can you move a little bit in that shape. It's difficult isn't it? Can you make just one arm into a straight line? Can you make your fingers into straight lines? etc.*

Good, now let's draw a funny shape. We'll pick up our crayons again and do a scribble squiggle like this. Let's do lots of scribbles all over the paper to scribble music! Now let's stand up over here away from the papers and we'll do scribbles with our whole self in the air. (Hands, heads, backs, knees, feet, etc., all move first together, and then as separate parts in a scribble action.) *Let's try and do that lying down. Now let's turn over the other way and do it again. I wonder if we can do kneeling down scribbles? How else can we do it?*

Now we'll do one more. Let's go back to our papers again and draw a circle, to the music ...... and another, and another, and another, etc. Now I wonder how we can make a moving circle with our bodies? (Examples to be offered might include spinning on the spot from either a standing, sitting, kneeling, or lying base; moving the arms round in circles from the shoulder joints; moving the head round in a circle, etc.) *Can you make some part of yourself into a "still" circle shape?* (Examples might include making a circle with finger and thumb; making a circle with the legs—bent knees turned outwards and soles of feet together; curling into a circle shape with the whole body in a sitting or lying position, etc.)

Don't be a perfectionist with the shapes made by the children, so long as they have got the right idea and are approximating them.

PIPE CLEANER SHAPES

The aim of this activity is similar to the aim in the drawing exercise, namely to clarify the concept of a shape visually before interpreting it with the body. In the drawing game, we made either still or moving shapes as seemed appropriate. In working with pipe cleaners, the shapes are quite often more complex, and a still version will suffice.

First, make a shape with a pipe cleaner and hold it up for the children to observe. Then ask them to make that shape with their bodies. Again, don't expect too much perfection. The convolutions of the knot (given below) obviously cannot be interpreted literally, but the idea of being "knotted" *can*.

The following shapes are suitable to make:

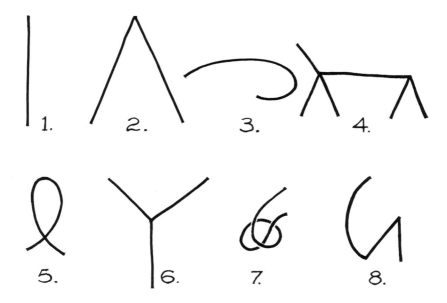

Children will come up with many different interpretations of the shapes, and turn them around in their minds in different directions. For example, no. 2 may be turned upside down by them, or else turned on its side. No. 6 may be interpreted with either arms or legs. No. 5 may be reproduced by crossing two fingers, arms, hands, or legs. A child might create No. 4 either on the back with arms and legs in the air, or standing like a horse with hands and feet on the floor.

Many new interpretations of a pipe cleaner shape may be offered, and it takes an alert mind to recognize them. (It's interesting to note that when a class of adults is given the same exercise, interpretations are more literal and less inventive.)

Knots

BLACKBOARD AND CHALK

These may, of course, be used for demonstrating simple shapes and provide an alternative to pipe cleaners, and paper and crayons.

MIRROR GAME

Another way of developing awareness of body shape through powers of observation, is to "mirror" the movements of another. This involves copying a slowly moving shape, and is the beginning of consciously making air patterns. The mirror idea is a device commonly used in many dance and movement classes, and the best way of implementing it with children in this young age group is to let the children be the mirror images by copying the teacher. The children should spread out in a line, horizontal to the teacher, with enough space around each one for freedom of movement.

I'm going to move very slowly and you can be the picture of me in my mirror. When I move my arm on this side slowly out to the side like this, you *move your arm on this side too.* (This means that when you move your right arm the children will be moving their left arms—but the words right and left are not used at this stage.) *Now you just follow me.* (Slow motion easy-to-follow movements in all directions with different parts of the body on a *stationary base* are then made by you with the children following. After a while ask for volunteers to come and take your place as the leader.)

Floor Patterns

CROSSING THE BRIDGE

(Described in the Section "Simple Patterns In Space", Chapter Six)

This game can again be played to encourage the idea of moving in a straight line, as well as to encourage innovation of movements. This time, however, each child can "cross the bridge" in turn, going across with one movement and back again with another. Each child should be encouraged to think up a new way of crossing the bridge.

A variation of this game can be played in a circle (Round the Tree) instead of in a straight line. As children this age have difficulty in making their floor pattern curve back to where they started, let them use a chair instead of an imaginary tree.

MOVING TOWARDS A FOCAL POINT AND AWAY FROM IT AGAIN

This can be done as explained in the preceding chapter (just after the section entitled "Crossing the Bridge), but now the children will have no adults to lead them. Place yourself, as at the center of a wheel, and let the children move in and out, as if they were moving along the spokes. As children like to bunch together, there will probably only be about three major spokes, unless you encourage them to make their separate journey on their own spoke. Of course, this means that there will be a widening space between themselves and their neighbors as they reach the periphery of the room. The younger ones won't be able to do it for a while, and it's best not to bother them too much with the idea, until they are old enough to understand.

Directions

The sense of moving from *side to side* and *forwards and backwards* may be encouraged by asking for examples of movements that can be done in these directions. Jumping, rocking, jumping with the feet while hands remain on the floor, walking on all fours (forward like a cat—sideways like a crab), are all suitable for side to side and backwards and forwards interpretation.

The story of the *Grandfather Clock* (told earlier on in this chapter in the section on Sensory Contrasts under the subheading "weight") is just as suitable for exploring different directions as it is for expressing differing gradations of weight. *The Broomstick Which Wouldn't be Good* (told later on in this chapter under the heading "More Stories and Poems") is also a good story for learning about directions.

UPWARDS AND DOWNWARDS

This has been partially dealt with under "Size and Contracting and Expanding" in the section on sensory contrasts. But it's useful to discover movements that can be directed upwards or downwards with different parts of the body as well as with the whole body. For example: pointing and reaching with the arm and finger up and then down; raising the back up towards the ceiling, then bringing it down as close to the floor as possible; standing on all fours and raising and lowering the neck and head; swinging the arms and upper body up then down; kicking a leg upwards then stamping it downwards, etc.

It's best not to confuse children with the concept of moving in two directions at once at this stage (for example moving up and down and from side to side at the same time). See the next chapter for this development.

Big or Little Spaces

The following are two movement games which enable the children to experience moving in a small space and then in a big one:

MOUSE IN THE HOUSE

Let's pretend we're each a tiny mouse in a tiny hole and we can only move round a little bit like this. (Shuffling round on the spot.) *Now let's poke our heads out of the hole and creep out. We've got the whole kitchen to move about in now. Let's creep all over the room—right across the middle—into the corners and across the room again. Now someone's coming! Quick, let's go back into our tiny hole where it's safe, even though we can't move much in there!*

The following is a movement game with hoops which are spread on the floor at a fair distance from one another. There should be at least as many hoops as children.

THE SEA AND THE ISLANDS

Let's pretend that we're in the sea swimming about (running between the hoops and moving the arms in a swimming motion). *Now there's a great big wave coming—can you hear it on the drum? Let's jump onto an island until it's gone. Find a hoop all to yourself and jump inside it.* (Drum roll or tambourine shake until the children have found a hoop.) *Let's run around the inside of our hoop as if we were running around our little island* (running accompaniment, gradually slowing down). *Now the sea is calm again, let's jump in and go for another swim, all between the hoops. This time when you hear the wave coming jump into the nearest hoop you can find. It doesn't matter if it's not the one you had last time.*

Some children are much slower than others at finding a hoop and may give up unless they are offered some assistance. Others are aggressive and try to "steal" hoops from others, so a certain amount of sorting out has to be done. As the children get used to finding a hoop, first one and then another hoop can be eliminated, so that the children now have to share hoops and therefore find themselves in a very small space on their islands. Make it clear when there is a change over from each child finding his own hoop to when they are supposed to share one if there aren't enough to go round. This part of the exercise is very much a social experience.

Our Own Space

It's very difficult for children of this age to find and maintain their own space, as they tend to converge through a desire to herd or a wish to be next to a friend. If asked to run and find a spot in the room where they are not close to anyone else, it usually turns into a game of "follow the leader" with a couple of children leading out into a new space, and the rest bunched up behind them. Where a concept fails, however, an imaginative idea works, and the following one is quite effective:

SWISHING WIND

Let's get a scarf and we'll pretend we're the wind blowing as we spin around in a circle . . . . . . we'll swish the scarf around us as we go. Make sure you have enough room to turn around without your scarf touching anyone else. You don't want to blow anyone else over!

Now let's see if you can move about all over the place, swishing your scarf in every direction, and still not touching anyone. Swish it from side to side, up and down, and now turn around again like a very wild wind, and still see if you have lots of room!

•Props

Scarves, hoops, mats, handpuppets, toys, are as useful for this age group as for the preceding one.

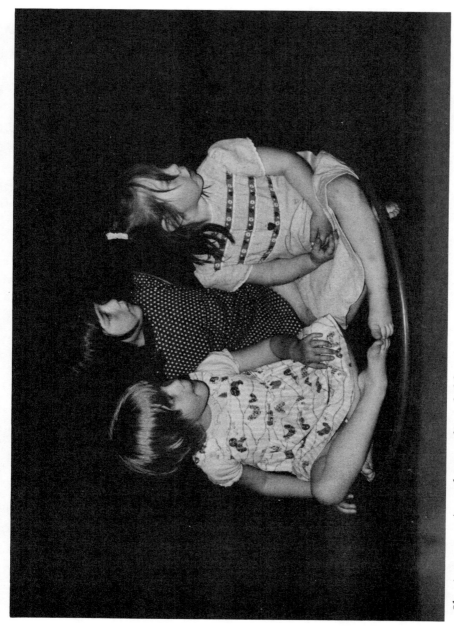

Sharing space (watching other children)

Jumping over coiled rope

A COILED UP ROPE

A coiled up rope may be used to jump over in as many ways as can be found, involving directions, shape, focus on different parts of the body, etc.

PICTURES

Pictures can sometimes set the scene for a fun make-up dance. e.g., clowns at the circus; kittens playing; a spaceship, etc.

BAG OF OBJECTS

Bring a bag of familiar objects and have each child in turn pull something out of it. Each object brought out is then observed for its different shape and sensory qualities. These sorts of questions may be asked:

What does it feel like?
What shape is it?
Is it light or heavy?
Is it hard or soft?
Does it bend or maybe snap in two?
How can we make it move?

The following are examples of suitable objects to bring and possible ways of interpreting them. Many others will no doubt come to mind.

Sharp pin	Sharp and straight hand, arm, leg, body movements
Soft fur	Stroking the air with hands, back, etc.
Crinkly tissues	Crinkling up different parts of body/ whole body
Incense smoke	Moving like wafting slowly drifting threads of smoke
Dinner knife	Straight, rigid shape, slicing through space in different ways
Nutcrackers	Making open Vee shape then squeezing together with arms, legs, hands, etc.
Pencil	"Writing" in space with hands, feet, heads, backs, etc.
Spool of thread	Rolling over and over without bending
Twig	Bending a little, then straightening
Rubber Band	Stretching and shrinking again in all directions
Cotton Wool	Lying still, lightly and softly

•Dancing with a Partner

Doing a dance holding hands with a partner helps a child to move in relationship to another. Some children are very good at matching their partner's pace and style; others find it hard to get going because they both want to do something different. Another couple will pull each other over, due to an excess of exuberance and force, while yet another will just stand and stare. Some children are always inclined to take the lead, and others to follow. For this reason it's a good idea to change partners two or three times during a partner dance. Two leaders and two followers may then have to sort things out. This is an exercise in cooperation.

Generally speaking, children very much enjoy doing a dance with someone else, but there may be one or two who just don't want to hold hands. In this case, let them dance on their own for the time being. In a few weeks they nearly always want to dance with a partner too. Some children have to be encouraged to "change" partners, because they want to stick with a friend, brother, or sister, and tact is needed. On one occasion a three and a half year old boy, who always came with a little girl neighbor, became outraged when she changed partners. "She can't dance with *him*," he said, pointing at her new partner, "she's my wife!"

SUITABLE PARTNER DANCES

Holding one hand—"Standing up" dance

Holding two hands—"Standing up" dance

Holding two hands—"On the floor" dance (e.g., sitting facing each other and rocking back and forth).

Holding a hoop

Crawling through a "tunnel" made first by one and then by the other (see Chapter 8, section "Dancing With a Partner," subsection "Under and Over," for the kind of tunnels which can be made).

Partner dance with hoop

•Listening

The art of listening can be consciously developed at this stage. An infant listens in a totally open way and all sounds seem to impinge on him with equal validity creating surprise, interest, and sometimes, fear. A baby's facial expression reveals the registering of many sounds which adults have ceased to "hear". As our environment is bombarded with an enormous variety of high level sound input, compared to that of our ancestors, we all too often learn to tune out as we grow up. However, our tuning out tends to be unselective—we often tune out both natural and mechanized sounds—the wind in the trees and the sounds of road repair; birdsong, and the incessant buzzing and humming of refrigerators and furnaces. But somehow the tuning out process is only partial; after all we have no flaps on our ears! We become accustomed to a constant, fairly undifferentiated level of sound as a background to living. Without this background many people feel on edge, hence their dependence on radios at work, and piped in music in public places.

The double effect of ceasing to register many sounds and needing a continuous background noise level, results in the anaesthetization of our listening capability. At three and a half, as the child interacts more and more with the environment, and as the acute yet passive hearing stage of the very young child is diminishing, it is important to preserve this listening response. In turn, this has a very direct effect on movement, and general body attitude.

It is only necessary to observe the sensitively alert body of a blind person sitting in a chair, or walking down a road, to recognize this connection. Or one may imagine a man walking along a forest path, listening for the rustle of animals in the bush. His whole body takes on an attitude of keen attention, of awareness, of being ready to move in any direction at need. By comparison, the movement of a youth who is walking down the road half listening to a transistor radio he carries is unmindful of his environment; his attention is inturned and he is quite unpoised for immediate action. In fact his body is no longer receptive to his surroundings.

The following "Listening and Doing" dance exercises train keenness of sound recognition, coordination of hearing and movement, and training of movement memory, through sound patterns.

The game of listening to sounds with the eyes closed (explained in the "Listening" Section of Chapter Six) may be played again, but instead of just listening to naturally occurring sounds, it is now useful for the teacher to make certain sounds—either vocally or on the percussion instruments or in any other way; (for example rattling a key ring; rustling a plastic bag; dropping three pennies; tearing a piece of paper). It's best to do this partially out of sight, as children get overcome by curiosity and will often peek!

When the children are asked to open their eyes and recall the sounds there will be a lot of right guesses. But if descriptions of imaginary sounds are still volunteered along with the descriptions of the "real" ones, it doesn't really matter as the attitude of listening will have been achieved.

The following activity not only develops listening sensitivity but trains the movement memory through the use of remembered sounds.

MIX-UP

Three percussion sounds are chosen, and the children volunteer suitable movements to go with each sound. *One* movement per sound is chosen from those volunteered. The prearranged movements are now practiced by the children and their corresponding sounds are played on the percussion instruments.

Some Examples are:

Percussion Sounds	*Corresponding Movements*
Tinging a triangle	Creeping on hands and feet
Shaking a tambourine	Spinning
Slowly beating a drum	Heavy stamping

After practicing, the sounds are played in a random order and the children try to match them with the right movements.

FREEZE

So far, the usual signals for stopping have been an extra loud percussion sound, or else a deliberate slowing of the music and a warning that the dance is going to come to an end. The reverse process can now be employed in the following game. The children are simply requested to *move in silence* and then to "freeze" when the music starts. The novelty of this approach results in much greater listening concentration, although conditioning will make it hard to do at first.

Children often tend to chatter to the detriment of both listening and movement. It is therefore useful to "Turn *off* our Voices" by turning off an imaginary switch in front of the mouth, and "Turn *on* our Ears" by turning on an imaginary switch in front of both ears.

With everybody's mouth turned off and ears turned on, it's now possible to teach several minutes of a class without anyone speaking (including you)! Eyes must observe and ears must listen. The quality of listening and general awareness is immediately enhanced, though usually five minutes is the longest one can go before a child forgets and says, "Do you know what?" or "Jimmy's pushing me!", etc.

A HAIKU
It is very beneficial for the children to listen to themselves dancing just as quietly as possible. The following Haiku gives an appropriate imaginative basis for this purpose.

NIGHT

Night drops so softly
I cannot hear the creeping
Shadows hide my house.

(A Haiku is traditionally Japanese and consists of a three lined nature poem with 5, 7, and 5 syllables respectively. It can provide excellent dancing material if it contains sufficient action. Brevity of idea and the feeling of the poetry readily translate into movement. The haikus in this book have been written specially for dancing by the author.) It may seem as if the above Haiku would be too sophisticated for four year olds to translate into movement, but it can first serve as the basis for an exchange of thoughts and feelings about darkness, shadows, and the quietness of nighttime. After being involved in such a discussion, the children really enjoy dancing to the idea.

This technique of evoking the children's responses to any suggested image will serve to bring out enthusiastic and imaginative interpretations in movement.

QUICK AS A FLICK

The following activity trains Ear-Muscle coordination which is often just as important as the more publicized Eye-Muscle coordination. The series of sounds used must *not* be rhythmical, but if possible should be sudden, disconnected, and arbitrary. When making the sounds, try not to let the children see when the percussion instruments are going to start and stop (maybe use a piece of furniture to mask your movement). Accompaniment may also be vocal. There must be at least as much silence as sound.

We're going to move to some sudden sounds. Whenever you hear a sound you move right away in any way you want, but when the sound stops—you stop to, just as quickly as you can!

•More Stories and Poems

MR. WIDDERSNOPPER

Once upon a time there was a tiny old man who lived in a bucket at the bottom of the garden. He was very bad and every morning he thought up all the bad things he could do that day. (Crouch in imaginary bucket.) *One morning it was raining like this.* (Drum with fingers on the floor.) *But after a while it stopped and the sun came out.*

Mr. Widdersnopper, who was very *naughty, said, "What can I do that's bad today?" He lifted his head and looked over the edge of the bucket.* (Rhythmically mime the rest of the actions as they occur in the story.) *Mrs. Brown was hanging out her clothes in the garden. "I know," said Mr. Widdersnopper, "I'll pull down Mrs. Brown's clothes off the line and make them all dirty."*

So he stepped out of his bucket, like this. SNIP SNAP SNOP. SNIP SNAP SNOP. (Clap and speak and stamp to each sound.) *When he got to the clothes line he jumped up to catch the sheet, like this, but it was too high.* (Jump several times—reaching with both arms together and then alternate arms.) *At last he got it—he pulled, pulled, and pulled!* (Strong tugging action.) *And he pulled, pulled, and pulled! At last he got it off the line.*

He dragged his hands in the dirt, like this...(Dragging action of hands on floor.) *Then he made the sheets all dirty.* (Wiping action just above the surface of the floor on imaginary sheets.) *He dragged his feet in the dirt like this.* (Dragging action of feet on the floor.) *Then he jumped all over the sheets like this.* (Fast aggressive jumping!)

"Now," he said, *"I'll put the sheet in the bird-bath!" He dragged it behind him across the wet grass. SNIP SNAP SNOP. SNIP SNAP SNOP. He then bundled it up into the bird-bath and sploshed all over it like this! After that he went back to the clothesline. SNIP SNAP SNOP. SNIP SNAP SNOP. He looked up at Mr. Brown's red shirt. Then he got a big long stick which was lying on the ground and reached up to the shirt, pulling it like this.* (Heavy, waving movement in the air.) *Down came the shirt! How do you think he got the shirt all dirty?* (Act on suggestions.) *Then he put the shirt on—it came right down to his ankles, and he lay down in the dirt and rolled and rolled and kicked and kicked and threw himself around in it!*

Then he stood up and did a leapy dance because he so much enjoyed being bad! After that he pulled the shirt off over his head and said, "I'll throw it over the fence into the next garden!" So he threw! But it didn't go high enough and fell back down again. And he threw! And he threw!

Guess what? It got stuck in the apple tree. Just then Mrs. Brown looked out of the window! "What *is my husband's shirt doing in the apple tree?" she said, "And* where *has my sheet gone? It must be that bad Mr. Widdersnopper!" And out she stomped, feeling very cross, just like this!*

Mr. Widdersnopper was still looking at the apple tree. "Mr. Widdersnopper—you are very bad!" He jumped with surprise. "You have messed up my nice clean clothes and now you will have to wash them!"

But Mr. Widdersnopper just looked more bad than ever. He stamped his feet and shook his fists and said, "No I won't! No I won't! No I won't!"

Then Mrs. Brown said slowly and firmly shaking her finger, "Yes you will!! Yes you will! Yes you will!"

Then Mr. Widdersnopper remembered that Mrs. Brown had a brand new washing machine, so he just said, "Hmmmmmm O.K." *He liked washing machines. So he carried the sheet and the shirt to the back door like this.* (Walk with bent knees and back as if carrying a wide load.) *SNIP SNAP SNOP! SNIP SNAP SNOP! He pushed them into the washing machine, poured in the soap and pushed the ON button. Then he watched them through a glass panel.*

Now we'll pretend to be the clothes in the washing machine. Here they are, lying in the bottom of the machine. (Limply lying.) *In comes the water and they all rise to the top like this.* (Drooping floating position.) *Then the clothes began to go up and down, up and down, up and down, up and down, round and round, round and round, round and round, round and round. After that the water came out quickly like this . . . . SHWWWWWWWWW! The clothes all sunk down again.*

Now it's time for the spin dry. Let's hold hands in a circle and run round faster and faster without pulling or letting go! Then the clothes slowed down again. (Rinse cycle can be tumbled and spun in the same kind of way.)

After that, Mrs. Brown said, "Good, now you can go home—and don't be be bad again for three days at least!"

Mr. Widdersnopper said, "Hmmmmmmmmmm! O.K." And off he went to his bucket. SNIP SNAP SNOP! SNIP SNAP SNOP! He climbed into his bucket and sat in the bottom wondering how to be bad again tomorrow—*he couldn't wait for three days! It started to rain again.* (Drum fingers on floor again.) *And he went to sleep.*

The following is a Halloween story and is very popular with all children between three and a half and six years old. It gives valuable practice in moving in different directions. It has the same kind of appeal as the Mr. Widdersnopper story, as the Broomstick is another "naughty" character! Some examples of the sort of verbal input classes can offer are given in the middle of the story.

THE BROOMSTICK THAT WOULDN'T BE GOOD

Once upon a time there was a witch. It was a week before Halloween and the witch wanted to practice with her broomstick to see if it was in good working order!

She walked in a hobbledy way, like this, over to her broomstick.

The broomstick stood all stiff and straight beside the wall. She opened her kitchen door and climbed on the broomstick. "Off you go!" she croaked.

"Wheeeeeeeeeeee!" said the Broomstick. But it started to go BACKWARDS. (Running backwards with legs apart.) *And the witch fell off!*

"Oh dear," said the witch, "There's something wrong here!" And she climbed on again. "Broomstick go through the door—don't go backwards any more!" she croaked.

"Wheeeeeeeeee!" said the Broomstick. But it started to go SIDEWAYS. (Galloping sideways with legs apart.) *And the witch fell off!*

"Oh dear," said the witch, "there's something wrong here!" And she climbed on again. "Broomstick go through the door—don't go sideways any more!" she croaked.

"Wheeeeeeeeee!" said the Brooomstick. But it started to go ROUND AND ROUND IN CIRCLES. And the witch fell off!

"Oh dear," said the witch, "this is a very difficult Broomstick!" And she climbed on again. "Broomstick go through the door—don't go round—not any more!" she croaked.

"Wheeeeee! Wheeeeeee! Wheeeeeee!" said the Broomstick, jumping forwards in SHORT SHARP JUMPS. *And the witch fell off!*

"Well, well!" said the witch getting up and rubbing her back. "I'm going to have to work a SPELL on you. You are certainly not in good working order!" And the witch picked up the Broomstick and walked with it in a hobbledy way over to her big black pot, which was called a cauldron.

Then she dropped the Broomstick into the boiling water and sprinkled in some special magic silver powder, like this. After that she said a spell in her croaky voice to make the Broomstick do as it was told. What do you think the words were that she made up?

(Two classes of four and a half year olds volunteered the following words after being given the two starting words, "Broomstick, Broomstick":

1) Broomstick Broomstick
   Wieners Wieners

Apple Pie . . . . You better be good!
2) Broomstick Broomstick
   You be good or else . . . . . .
   I'll turn you into something different—
   See?
We solemnly chanted the above words to a rising crescendo three times while stirring the pot!)

Then the witch took the Broomstick from the pot. It was glittering silver. She walked over to the door in a hobbledy way and climbed onto the Broomstick, saying, "Don't be silly any more—go straight forwards through the door!" in a croaky voice. And the Broomstick did!

It said, "Wheeeeeeeeeee!" and shot straight forwards into the night, like this. Over the trees it went—over the houses, over the roads, over the fields it went . . . . . .BUT—IT WOULDN'T STOP! And the witch fell off! She was mad as mad as mad could be—but the Broomstick kept on going! Then she gave a great big leap and grabbed at it as it turned round and sailed past her. She missed it! She started to run after it in a hobbledy way and gave a great big leap again. She caught it by the end, and the Broomstick dragged her all the way home again!

"Oh dear!" said the witch in a croaky voice, rubbing her back, "You are still not in good working order. I will have to work another spell on you! So the witch dropped her Broomstick into the cauldron again. This time she sprinkled in some special magic golden powder, like this. Now what were the words she used in the spell this time?

(Group No. 1's response was to reverse their spell thus:
       You better be good....Apple Pie
       Wieners Wieners
       Broomstick Broomstick!
This set a precedent and now the story always gives the Stopping spell as the reverse of the Going spell.)

The witch lifted her Broomstick out of the pot and it came out glittering golden. She walked over to the kitchen door in a hobbledy way, saying "Broomstick you may go once more—but come back to my kitchen door!" in a croaky voice. And she climbed on again. THIS TIME THE BROOMSTICK DID AS IT WAS TOLD!

It said, "Wheeeeeeeeee!" and shot off into the night. Then it turned round, slowed down, and stopped by the kitchen door.

"Well **that** *seems to be in good working order, at last," croaked the witch. She walked to the wall in a hobbledy way and put the Broomstick there again. It stood straight and stiff, but it was sparkling with golden light. (Vibratory movements all over.) "You're too excited," said the witch, "you've still got a few days to wait until Halloween. CALM DOWN. CALM DOWN. CALM DOWN," she said in a croaky voice, waving her hands down, down, down, down, down. And the Broomstick just quietly glowed—waiting! But the witch was so tired that she just fell asleep for a while.*

This next story brings out the sense of both restricted and free movement. Because different movements in the story are associated with specific musical sounds, it can be repeated in its musical form with as few words as are needed to prompt the action. This, of course, improves movement memory.

THE CATERPILLAR

Once there was a caterpillar egg laid upon a leaf. It was quite still. The leaf seemed like all the world to it. Then, as it felt the warm sun, it began to wiggle. And as it wiggled slowly, it grew longer with little bumps sticking off it that it could walk on. So it moved its tail end up to its head and humped its back—this way. Then it stretched forward and flattened out again—for that is the way a caterpillar walks. After a bit it lay still and then curled around on its side to look at itself. Then it curled around on the other side. It looked just the same on both sides! Then off it went for a walk again.

It humped and flattened and humped and flattened, and explored the space all around it. It walked right off the leaf which had been its whole world, and into a new world of grass and earth. It explored and explored and explored all over the place.

Now one day, the caterpillar got sick of walking in all this space and started to make a little nest or cocoon to rest in, hanging from two twigs. It moved its head back and forth this way, weaving a white sticky thread around itself until it was quite closed in. Now it had made another tiny world to curl up and rest in because it was very tired. It waited, and while it was all still and curled, a wonderful thing began to happen. It began to change its shape!

One very hot day it began to move again. It wanted to get out of this tiny cocoon world. It had been there long enough. So it pushed with its head against the end of the cocoon. It pushed and pushed. Out came its head. The sun was very bright. It waited a while, then slowly crawled out.

Then it felt two things on the side of itself which hadn't been there before. It stretched and the two things on either side stretched out too. Somehow it felt very new and different. What do you think had happened to the caterpillar? Yes, it had turned into a butterfly and grown two beautiful wings. It started to wave them up and down, up and down. They were blue and orange with fine brown lines across them. Then without knowing how it had happened, it had lifted off into the air. This was like being in another world again. It was flying through bright space and felt very light and free. The butterfly brushed against a flower and landed there for a minute or two, its wings folded high on its back. Now what was that bright, hot, wonderful thing up there? The butterfly would try and reach it. It flew up, up, up, fluttering towards the sun.

Now, let's do the story again this way:

Separate sounds must be found on percussion or accompanying instruments for the following movements:

Wiggling — when egg starts to turn into a caterpillar
Walking — humping and flattening
Weaving — making a cocoon
Resting — lying inside the cocoon
Pushing — trying to get out of the cocoon
Flying — fluttering through the air

We'll go through the movements the caterpillar made with the special sounds again. This time I won't tell you the whole story but I'll just give the name of the movements—This is the wiggling sound...let's all wiggle to it. This is the walking sound...let's all do a caterpillar walk to it. This is the weaving sound, etc. Now we'll listen to the story again and the special sounds will help you to re-member what movement to do. Can you help me tell the story this time? How did it begin?

Do children still like to pretend to be Princes and Princesses who live in castles with winding dark staircases? Yes they do! This is one of the most popular movement stories.

This version of the story is told from the point of view of the Prin-cess to avoid saying "The Prince and Princess" and pluralizing the activities each time.

THE PRINCESS AND THE TOYS

Once upon a time there was a Princess who lived in a castle way up on a hill. But she was unhappy because she had no toys to play with. One day when she was eating her porridge by herself she started to feel very unhappy indeed. She didn't know whether to cry or to get angry. So she decided to get angry! She banged down her golden spoon on her porridge plate . . . CRASH! Let's do that again . . . CRASH! Now let's do that as hard as we can with both hands . . . CRASH! Then she said, "I shall go exploring today. I shall go up those funny little stairs at the back of the castle where no one has been for such a long time, and see what's at the top."

So she crept through the kitchen on tippy-toe and out into the big hall. There was a doggy asleep in the big hall and she had to go past it very quietly so as not to wake it up. See if you can tread so quietly that your feet make no noise at all. Just as she was passing the doggy it twitched its nose and growled in its sleep. She froze and stayed ever so still. Then in a minute she crept to the bottom of the little staircase. She looked one way, then the other way. Then she did it again. No one was there.

Up she went (Knees lifted high.) She went up and up and up and up and it got darker and darker so that she had to feel her way with her hands in front of her. At last she got to the top! It was quite dark now. She felt around and there were lots of cobwebs. She was in a little passageway. She took little tiny steps with her hands in front of her face so as not to bump herself. BUMP! Her hands touched a door.

There was an old, heavy knob on the door. She turned it. (Rasping sound with voice and turning action with hand.) *It was stiff. She pushed on the door. It would not open. She pushed harder. It still would not open. She pushed and pushed and pushed so hard—WUMPH! The door opened suddenly and she fell through onto the floor. Now we know what we're doing let's do that again. Push, push, push, push, push—WUMPH!*

She found herself on the floor of a little room right at the top of the castle. In the middle of the room was a box. Let's lift the lid of the box. It's very, very heavy. L-I-F-T! . . . and it dropped shut again. Let's do that again. L-I-F-T! Oh dear it's fallen shut again. This time we must be just as strong as we can be. L-I-F-T! *Oh good . . . this time it's stayed open. Now what's inside it? Why it's full of toys! But these are no ordinary toys. They can speak!*

A little voice said, "Pick me up!" It was a rubber ball. The Princess picked it up. Then it squeaked, "Bounce me!" So the Princess bounced it all over the place. BOUNCE BOUNCE BOUNCE. (Bouncing action first with one hand, then with the other, then with both, while bouncing whole body in a jump.) *After a while the ball said, "Roll over and over with me!" So the Princess did. Then it squeaked, "Throw me up in the air and catch me!" So the Princess did that too, lots of times . . . . . . up and down . . . up and down . . . up and down.*

Just then another voice came out of the box. "What about me?" *She looked over the edge and there was a small blue squidge of squishy stuff. What could it be? It said, "Roll me into a ball!" So she did.* (Roll one hand over the other.) *It said, "Stretch me out!"* (Expanding movement with arms out sideways, and repeating with diagonal stretches at different angles to the floor.) *Then it said, "Squish me up!" So she squished it together again.* (Compressing hands together.) *What do you think the blue squishy stuff was? That's right—it was play-dough! Well the play-dough said, "Now you* do *all that. You roll into a ball!"* (Whole body action—crouching and turning around on the spot.) *"You stretch out!"* (Stretching

in various directions with whole body, including legs and spine.)
"You *Squish yourself up!"* (Contracting with whole body inwards
and downwards.)

*PLOP! Something fell out of the toy box. It was a floppy doll with
arms and legs made of cloth. They just went flop, flop, like this.
"Do a dance with me!" said the floppy doll. So the Princess did.
They both flopped their whole selves all over the place and then fell
down in a heap.*

KNOCK KNOCK KNOCK! Something was banging on the inside
*of the box. The Princess looked in, and there was a little wooden
doll with* stiff *arms and legs trying to get out. She lifted it out and it
said, "Now it's* my *turn!" So she did a stiff dance with the wooden
doll all over the room until the wooden doll was tired and had to
sit down. It's hard to sit down stiffly.* You *try it. K-Plomple! You
have to fall down the last bit don't you?*

(At this point many different kinds of toys can speak, move, and
get the Princess to move in their way. Examples: A toy airplane; a
train; a spinning top; a jack-in-the-box, etc. When the children's attention begins to waver, then bring in the next section of the story):

What's that noise? Someone *is coming up the stairs. THUMP
THUMP THUMP THUMP THUMP! It was the King! Let's pick up
all the toys and put them back in the box very quickly. Now we'll
hide down behind the box so we can't be seen. THUMP THUMP
THUMP THUMP THUMP!* (While the children hide behind the box
you can mime the King coming up the stairs.) *The King looks in
through the door and shakes his head. "Why, bless me there's nobody there!" he says, and he turns round and goes all the way down
the stairs again. THUMP THUMP THUMP!*

Now you *all pretend that you're the King and* I'll *stay behind the
box.* (Children now thump around you and pretend to open the door
and look in, while you crouch down and pretend to be behind the
box. It gives them practice in moving without your lead.) *THUMP
THUMP THUMP!* (Have them speak the words of the King if they
can remember them.)

*Well, when the King had gone, the Princess climbed out from
behind the box and took just one toy with her. She knew the other*

Jack-in-the-box (learning how to spring)

toys would be there when she wanted them. Which toy will you take? O.K. Let's go down the stairs again now. (Return journey reversing the incidents of the way there.)

When the Princess crept into the kitchen on tippy-toe, she saw that her porridge hadn't been cleared away. So she just sat down and finished it with her golden spoon. But she wasn't sad or angry any more because now she had a toy to play with like other boys and girls.

The following poem of Mr. Hoppity (or Mrs. Hoppity) and the Shoes, can first of all be spoken while the children are listening quietly, and then translated into a story version which is danced during the narration, as the other stories are.

MR. HOPPITY AND THE SHOES

Old Mr. Hoppity wants some shoes
But he doesn't know which are the ones to choose.
Some are too tight, and some are too floppy;
Some are too heavy and draggy and droppy;
Some are too movey and some are too stoppy!
But one is just right to go hippity hoppy.
What will he do with only one shoe?
Let's make him another one, sew him a brother one,
So he can hippity hoppit on two!

Here is Mr. Hoppity lying in bed very early on a cold winter's morning. The blankets are right off his feet and his feet are very very cold. He wakes up and shakes his cold feet in the air like this! But it doesn't do any good. So he sits up in bed and rubs his feet. But that *doesn't do any good. So he stands up and looks at his old slippers. But* that *doesn't do any good either because his old slippers are all worn through.*

"What shall I do?" said Mr. Hoppity. "I know, I'll go along to the shoe shop down the road, and see if there are any shoes that will fit me." So he went down the stairs and out into the street.

It was snowing. The snow was coming down very lightly. Let's dance the way the snowflakes twisted round and round, floating to the ground. Mr. Hoppity was so cold in his bare feet in the snow, he

had to run all the way to the shoe shop. When he got there, he
jumped up and down to try and warm up his feet, then he peeked in
through the window. no one was there, but the light was on. So he
banged on the door, three times. KNOCK KNOCK KNOCK! . . . . . .
Nobody came. He banged on the door with the other hand, three
times, KNOCK KNOCK KNOCK! But nobody came. He banged on
the door three times with both hands KNOCK KNOCK KNOCK.
Shall we do that again just as hard as we can! KNOCK KNOCK
KNOCK! Now let's do it jumping up and down at the same time,
KNOCK, KNOCK KNOCK! . . . Still nobody came. "Then I'll have
to go inside," said Mr. Hoppity.

This was a magic shoe shop. In the middle on the floor was a big
pile of colored shoes. He sat on the floor and looked at all the lovely
shoes. First he picked up a blue pair and put them on his feet. But
there was something wrong with them . . . they were too small and
tight, and his toes all curled up like this. When he stood up, he
curled all up—his back, his hands, his neck, and his knees, because
he felt too tight all over. And he did a funny too tight walk like this.
"Well that's no good," said Mr. Hoppity, and he sat down, pulled
off the shoes—and looked for another pair.

Then he picked up a lovely yellow pair and put them on his feet.
But there was something wrong with these shoes too. They seemed
too big and floppy. Flop, flop, flop, flop, went his feet. When he
stood up the whole of him began to go flop, flop, flop, flop—his
arms, hands, head, shoulders, tummy . . . and he floppity flopped all
around the shoe shop. "Well that's no good," said Mr. Hoppity, and
he kicked one of the floppy shoes off. KICK—up in the air it went.
He kicked the other floppy shoe off. KICK—up in the air it went. He
liked kicking so he gave a few more kicks . . . KICK KICK KICK
KICK KICK! It helped to get his feet warm!

Then he picked up a beautiful red pair and put them on his feet.
They seemed to fit all right, but when he tried to move, goodness
gracious, they were too heavy and draggy and droppy! The only
way Mr. Hoppity could move was to put his hands down on the
floor and drag his feet behind him like this. "Well that's no good,"
said Mr. Hoppity, and he stepped out of those heavy, draggy, droppy
shoes and looked for another pair.

The next shoes he found were orange and they were very funny.

As soon as he put one on his foot, his foot started to move all over the place. Quickly, quickly it shook up and down, and it wouldn't stop! So he put on the other shoe, and that one moved quickly quickly too. His feet were just shaking all over the place and wouldn't stop. So Mr. Hoppity stood up, and his feet took off and ran, ran, ran, ran, ran, ran, ran, all over the shoe shop, quickly quickly. "Help, help!" he said, and sat down again . . . . . . but his shoes kept on going. So Mr. Hoppity took the shoes off his feet and put them on his hands instead. Then his hands moved ever so quickly, like this. So Mr. Hoppity took the shoes off his hands and put them on his head. Then his head moved ever so quickly, like this. So Mr. Hoppity took the shoes off his head and put them on his knees. Then his knees moved ever so quickly, too. Then he knelt down and put them on his back, and his back wriggled and wiggled from side to side, ever so quickly, too. "Help!" said Mr. Hoppity again . . . and he took them off altogether and put them on the floor. At last the shoes stopped moving!

Mr. Hoppity was feeling quite tired by now. "I think I'll look for a nice still pair of shoes, now," he said. He picked out a brown pair and tried them on. They seemed to fit him quite well. He stood up, but do you know, he couldn't move his feet at all. They were stuck to the floor! Now let's all say to our feet, "FEET—STAY THERE!" Are you ready? "FEET-STAY THERE!" Now we'll see what Mr. Hoppity did. He tried to move his body this way, and that way. He moved his body in all the ways he could while his feet stayed stuck to the floor. He moved his tummy this way and that way; he moved his seat this way and that way; he moved his shoulders up and down; he moved his head from side to side; he swung his arms across his body from side to side; he bent his knees up and down; he twisted his whole self from side to side. What other ways could Mr. Hoppity Move? (Act out the class suggestions.) *After all that . . . still he couldn't move those shoes. So he stepped right out of them, saying, "Well* that's no good." *And he sat down again.*

There was only one shoe left now. What color was it? Oh all right, it was a shiny green one. It was a beautiful fit—there was nothing wrong with this *shoe. But what can you do in one shoe? That's right—you can hop.* (A few seconds of hopping.) *Now let's put the shoe on the other foot and hop on* that *one. After a bit, Mr.*

Hoppity found the foot he was hopping on got tired. "Well that's no good," he said. And he sat down again.

What can we do to help him? I know, let's make him another green shiny shoe, so that he can have two. Let's pretend we have a nice big green shiny piece of leather here, and we're going to go SNIP SNIP SNIP round the leather with a pair of scissors. SNIP SNIP SNIP. Now we'll get a needle out of this pin-cushion here, and we'll thread it carefully—like this—with green thread. Now we'll SEW and SEW and SEW and SEW. Do you think it will fit him? Let's break off the thread—SNAP! and pop the needle back in the pin-cushion.

Now Mr. Hoppity tries on the shoe we have made him. Oh, it fits him perfectly! He has two beautiful green shiny shoes! He puts his hand in his pocket and pulls out some pennies and puts them on the table of the magic shoe shop, to pay for the shoes. Then he's so pleased that he just jumps all over the place! He goes out of the shoe shop, shuts the door, and dances all the way home in the snow.

When he gets home he's so tired with all the shoe dancing that he takes off his lovely green shoes, puts them under his pillow, and goes to sleep. But this time when he wakes up, he will have a warm new pair of shoes to put on.

Perhaps you'd like to keep your eyes closed with Mr. Hoppity and have a little rest.

•Dividing the Material into Lessons

The material contained in this chapter is at least enough for one year of dancing lessons. Three quarters of an hour is a good lesson length. Repetition is needed, but not as much as in the preceding age group. New angles and twists can constantly be added to familiar material, and these are often prompted by the children's reactions.

Each week it is desirable to start and end with circle activities, to have one story or poem, and to do an exercise in which each child offers a short "solo", if willing, (for example in The Magic Dance, Our Own Dance, or Crossing the Bridge).

Other activities may be dipped into as required—two or three topics should be pursued within the course of a lesson (for example, a sensory contrast, a use of space, an exercise in listening and doing, etc.). Each area should be developed more surely and deeply as the weeks go by. The approach in general is similar to that of caring for a plant—"Water as needed."

Once again, a lesson plan is a very useful tool and reminder, but one of its main uses is the thought and reflection it provokes, while it is being drawn up, regarding the children's needs.

CHAPTER EIGHT

STAGE THREE—FROM ABOUT FOUR AND A HALF TO SIX YEARS OLD INCLUSIVE

•General Description

> *Two things are necessary: the development of individuality and the participation of the individual in a truly social life.*
>
> —*Maria Montessori*

At this stage children have a more defined image of their environment and are better able to reflect on it. Their constantly developing body image makes it easier for them to be aware of space and time relationships outside themselves. These in turn develop their body image more fully and clearly. Outer and inner perspectives are thus interdependent and children are better able to translate thought into movement and movement into thought. This means that they now have a better basis for creativity. Jean Piaget, in his essay "The Mental Development of the Child," has this to say: " . . . the progress of sensorimotor intelligence leads to the construction of an objective universe in which the subject's own body is an element among others. . . . The elaboration of space is essentially derived from the coordination of movements so that there is a direct relationship between the development of a sense of space and of sensorimotor intelligence."

As true creative dancing begins to emerge, more complex and exciting things can be done, and children can play a greater role in developing ideas.

Socially, at this stage, children are better able to cooperate with a partner or a small group, and more dances can be done which require interaction with others.

Verbally, children have a much wider vocabulary than they had a year ago and words can thus be used more effectively as a tool.

While a lot of the material from the preceding chapter is still relevant, it can be presented with less demonstration. This gives more opportunity for divergent response within the given framework. The encouragement of this individual response is a primary aim in teaching creative dance to this age group. And the *primary attitude* to be evoked is a sense of adventure!

Children who are involved, enthusiastic, and self motivated when creating dance at the age of five and six, have a good general grounding in the creative approach towards life and learning at *any* age.

•Circle Activities

Rhythm Activities

Clapping a variety of rhythms while vocalizing and possibly moving in some other way as well, provides a challenge in rhythm and coordination. For example one could clap and rock the head from side to side while saying, "Blueberry Pie; Blueberry Pie; Soft Ice Cream and Blueberry Pie." Another suitable phrase could be, "How about a Doughnut, a Doughnut, a Doughnut? How about a Doughnut?—a Jam One for Me!"

INDIVIDUAL CLAPPING PATTERNS

Sometimes it's useful to give "clap back" rhythms. If you are wondering how to come up with a suitable rhythm, the first line of a nursery rhyme often provides just the right amount of challenge, such as, "Inky Winky Spider"; "Mary had a Little Lamb"; "Sing a Song of Sixpence"; "Ding Dong Bell, Pussy's in the Well." Just think the words in your head as you clap the rhythm twice, slowly, then ask a child to clap back the rhythm as accurately as possible. Just give as many rhythms to clap back as interest warrants per week. Eventually everyone will get turns. In this way you can keep tabs on the rhythm development of each child.

Those who have not developed some sense of rhythm at this stage because they have not had the opportunity for the right growing experiences in the area of rhythm are noticeably less expressive in dance, even though they may be inventive and agile. It is as though rhythm not only aids in the creation of form, but that it is a vital key to liberating personality and feelings through physical expression.

SONG OF THE ROBOT

This rhythm game involves two, three, and eventually four sound patterns being spoken by groups of children at the same time. The following is a typical robot song.

First there is a basic beat — *1* 2 3 4 to which one says BONG (holding the "Ng" sound to the end of the 4 beats); then there are different divisions of the basic beat as follows: *1* 2 3 4 to which one says BIM BAM (2 beats each); *1 2 3 4* to which one says BEEP BEEP BEEP BEEP (1 beat each); and then, if the children can manage it, 1 and 2 and 3 and 4 and, to which one says CHUPA CHUPA CHUPA CHUPA (½ a beat to each syllable).

Everyone speaks each rhythm in unison at first, to become familiarized with the idea. When the sounds are familiar, divide the group into two and have half speak BONG, while the other half says BIM BAM. When the children can keep this duet going in time, try introducing a third group saying BEEP BEEP BEEP BEEP. *Only* when this is clear and rhythmic, introduce CHUPA CHUPA CHUPA CHUPA as well. You may not get any further than BIM BAM with some groups, but it doesn't matter!

Eventually, some simple action can accompany each sound. For example: BIM BAM—shrugging shoulders up then down; BEEP BEEP BEEP BEEP—pointing alternate index fingers past ears to the ceiling.

PERCUSSION

In addition to keeping time in the circle with percussion instruments handed out to the class, sometimes choose individual children to "help" you keep time when the rest are doing a dance, either within the circle, or round the room. This enables you to monitor their sense of rhythm again. If a few of the children are really off the beat it won't matter too much from the point of view of the dancing children as long as you are prepared to make more sound on your percussion instrument than your helpers do.

Locating different parts of the body

First of all let the children watch and follow you as fast as they can, (speed eye-muscle coordination), as you touch eyes, back, tummy, chest, knees, feet, head, shoulders, etc. Then try a few more complicated maneuvers such as: one hand on shoulder, other on elbow—reverse; one arm round back of head with hand over ear, other arm in front of face with hand over other ear—reverse; one hand on head, other hand on tummy—reverse, etc.

Secondly speak the actions without demonstrating them (speed ear-muscle coordination). It will take children longer to locate the correct part of the body when they don't have a picture to follow, and when they have to formulate the image in their brains.

Thirdly, go around the circle asking each child to name a body part in turn and touch it at the same time. Everyone follows each child by naming and touching the same part. This method takes longer still as the lead child has first to make a choice, then to visualize and name it while touching the right part of himself at the same time. Often a child will omit the naming process, unless reminded.

PAINT POT

This game from Chapter Seven in the section on Circle Activities, under the subheading "Locating Different Parts of the Body" can be repeated. Then try dipping *two* parts of the body into the imaginary paint, after which make up a dance specially using those parts. For example, the head and one hand, or the shoulders and the knees. This enhances coordination.

Training Speed of Response

"HOT"—A CIRCLE GAME

In the previous chapter, the children slowly reached forward first with hands, then feet, then heads, into the center of the circle. Then to the cue of a loud percussive sound they quickly withdrew the extended part, as if they had touched something hot.

Now many other parts of the body can be used in addition, one at a time, from different starting positions: elbows, shoulders, chests, tummies, hips, sides, plus any other parts of the body suggested by the children, can be extended slowly into the center of the circle *from sitting, kneeling, and standing positions. On signal, the extended part of the body is rapidly brought back to the normal position with a quick muscular contraction. Really excellent percussive movement develops from this game.*

Singing activities

At this stage you can help children learn to sing in tune by humming them a single note and asking them to hum it back to you opening it up into a vowel. For example,

Mmmmmmmmmm—Aaaaaaaaa

Mmmmmmmmmm—Eeeeeeeee .

Mmmmmmmmmm—Ooooooooo

The first note of the song should then be established in the same way before going ahead, as otherwise children tend to start on any note and plough their way rather tunelessly through a confusion of sound. Most children seem to be able to learn to pitch a note correctly in due course. Some can do it immediately, others take several weeks.

Any nursery rhyme or popular children's song can be used at this point. Children seem quick to learn the words and tunes of those songs which are new to them. Qualities of dancing can also be evoked in song, as suggested previously. Slow/fast, quiet/loud, sudden/sustained, high/low contrasts can be used. Appropriate hand-arm gestures may be added, as if the child were conducting.

Just as children like to create dances, they also like to create songs. When asked to do so they will often begin to "sing a story" as the ancient balladeers and minstrels used to do.

"Our own dance" in the circle

The comments on this activity in the previous chapter are also pertinent to this age group. In addition one may ask children of four and a half and up *not to copy* what anyone else has just done. This encourages innovation while training observation and memory.

Dancing *with the eyes closed* may also be done, one by one in the circle. Give the children a demonstration by dancing in the middle with your eyes closed yourself. Then tell them that you will be beside them to say "stop" right away if they are going to bump into anyone or fall over. (Keep close to them so that you can *catch* them

Own dance

if necessary.) Then ask for volunteers. Most children will want to have a turn. This exercise helps to develop the kinesthetic sense.

•Using the Space of the Whole Room including On the Floor Dances

THE MAGIC DANCE

The Magic Dance described in the previous chapter under the same heading ("Using the Space of the Whole Room," etc.) is still a great favorite. As a variation you can ask the whole group if they can move across the floor in a difficult position. For example moving along lying on their sides with only one of their hands in contact with the floor, or moving along sitting down with both their feet off the floor. It is amazing how much originality and variety of movement can be produced from this simple format. Now volunteers can demonstrate their versions to the rest of the class, and the children can try out the ways of moving that are demonstrated. This increases everyone's vocabulary of movement.

ANIMALS

It's now possible to embark on group projects. Divide the class into three or four groups, and should there be any adult assistants, they can be assigned as group advisors. If there are none, you will have to act as general advisor to each group in turn; but it's important to let children contribute their own ideas so that it's a shared project rather than one in which they are simply told what to do.

Each group then chooses a creature to enact in movement (for example, the children in one group could be kangaroos, in another group spiders, in a third group snakes, etc.) Each group then decides on a formation in which to move (for example, in a line behind a leader, across the room at random, in a circle, one at a time down the room, etc.) One by one the groups then demonstrate. It should take at least 20 seconds to carry out the task and fully depict the movement or movements involved. (A cat may both spring and creep; a rabbit may both hop and thump on the ground with its back feet!) The children who are watching then guess what creature is being depicted.

Discussion can then take place on how each group could make it easier for the rest to guess what creature they have chosen. For example (as discussed in the last chapter) most children won't make much differentiation at first between kangaroos, rabbits, and frogs. They often know what they are doing inside of themselves but don't realize that they may not be communicating it in movement. Communication in movement, as in speech, takes much practice, which this type of exercise helps to provide.

•Sensory Contrasts and Sensory Combinations

Up to the age of about three and a half, imitation provided the means for developing contrasts in qualities of movement. Up to the age of about four and a half, this system was augmented by different movement games, using imagery as a basis.

The sensory contrasts which were at first extracted one by one for practice and exploration (high/low, light/heavy, fast/slow, etc.) now tend to blend into a range containing more subtle differentiations, as well as appearing more frequently in combination. For example, a dance depicting a wind storm could utilize both moments of stillness and moments of intense motion, many gradations of speed, both sustained and sudden movements, light and heavy movements, high, low, and middle movements, and would generally tend towards abandoned (rather than controlled) and relaxed (rather than stiff) movements.

In other words, the movement vocabulary which has gradually been built up is now being utilized to form descriptive passages. Instead of saying, "Now we'll do a very light dance on our toes, like this," as one might to three year olds, or, "Show me how the leaves are falling," as one might to four year olds, one could now deal with the following Haiku for dancing.

LOGS AND SEAWEED
Logs and brown seaweed
Are tossed from the tumbling tide
Onto the hot sand.

Do you think the seaweed is light or heavy? Does it float slowly or quickly? Does it move up and down with the waves? How else do you think it moves? Show Me! Yes, it can go from side to side as well. Do the logs move in a different way from the seaweed? Show me how they move? How do you think they get up onto the sand? What does "tumbling" mean? Can you show me how waves tumble! (Etc.)

Gradually a picture emerges from asking questions about a basic idea. Clues are researched, children are reminded of the range and variety of movement that is possible. Then guided practice of this or that part of the idea follows before putting it all together into a dance. It's important to remember that children still cannot retain a complex idea in their heads, so the aim should be towards clarity and simplicity.

The process involved in writing a word, a paragraph, and then a story, is parallel to the process involved in mastering a movement, a series of interconnected movements, and then a dance. The story and the dance are both dependent on mind and skill development to the point where form, meaning, and expression meet. But guided practice time, which is analogous to the scales, arpeggios, and studies of a pianist, remain the essential backbone of every class. It may have a direct bearing on a particular theme to be danced, as in the above example of logs and seaweed, or it may simply be general practice for the development of movement skills to be used in a later context. In addition to the sensory contrast activities of the last chapter (don't be afraid to repeat) here are some more, some of which involve working with a partner or a group.

Tempo

CLOUDS

This activity involves moving alone, in a group, then alone again, and there are varying gradations of speed. The movement is generally flowing and sustained.

Find a space where you can be by yourself. Can you show me how a cloud moves? Try bending your knees, letting your arms float out and swaying about very gently as you slowly move along.

Now, as you move about hold a hand with whoever is near you. Slowly float about together and join onto some more people. Now you're helping to make a bigger cloud. Remember to move slowly . . . let's slowly drift the clouds together until we're all holding hands. Now we're making one very big cloud! Remember to sway about, leaning to one side, and then the other, but don't pull each other over! Let's pretend the wind comes along and blows our cloud faster—it starts to twist around as we're blown along. Keep holding hands.

Now the cloud gets all heavy with rain waiting to fall out. Bend your knees more and let yourself go all droopy as the whole circle moves. The rain is coming . . . pit - pat - pit - pat . . . our cloud starts to let the rain out. Let go hands, put your arms above your heads and drop quickly to the ground like rain - SWOOSH SWOOSH SWOOSH! Have you all dropped?

Just stay lying there and listen to the rain sounds on the tambourine . . . see if the sound makes a picture of the rain for you. Now the rain is stopping, the sounds are coming more and more slowly now. The sun comes out.

Now a mist starts to rise up off the ground. Let's slowly start to move like the mist, floating up, up, up, and all around in the air again, arms stretched out, knees bent, swaying about like this. Now you are moving like the clouds at the beginning again.

Let's keep going and do it all over again. It should be easier this time. Do it by yourselves without my joining in the dance. . . . I'll just speak the words for you.

N.B. Tasks such as the above one are within the mental and physical grasp of most children in this age group. However, the ability to cooperate socially, or the ability to maintain concentration when working with a group or a partner, may not be sufficiently developed in some. The factor of social maturity must be reckoned with when deciding whether to do a certain partner or group exercise.

FLY IN A FLUSTER

Do you know what it means to be in a fluster? It means to feel all bothered and in a great hurry. A fly feels in a fluster when it is rushing about trying to get out of the kitchen. It goes Bzzzzzzzzzz

Bzzzzzzzzzzzz Bzzzzzzzzzz —and the more it rushes about, the harder it seems to be to get out, so the fly gets cross and upset.

Let's move like a fly in a fluster. We'll pretend we're whizzing about the kitchen—rushing across the room and back very fast—but look where you're going! Every time I bang my drum, change your direction very quickly and don't crash into any other flies! (Long whizzing movements across the floor, with sharp changes of direction on the drum beat.)

Now flies, STOP! (Extra loud bang on drum.) *We'll pretend we've landed on a window. The window goes up and down instead of across, like the floor. The fly is getting tired and it turns around on its feet like this. Do you know how many feet a fly has? Six, that's right. Well we can look as if we have four, with our two hands and two feet, and we'll just have to pretend that we have the two extra ones! Now we'll turn round a little bit on this pretend window straight up in front of us, then we'll turn back again. Now we'll turn round a little bit to the other side, then we'll turn back again. Let's stay still for a few seconds. wait for the tambourine to shake, then off you go whizzing again.* (Repeat sequence.)

Now this time we'll go for a little slow walk on the window. The fly is getting really tired—it isn't in a fluster any more—it just feels so weary. Suddenly it walks round the edge of the window! What a surprise—off it floats into the air! (This is also an exercise in changing direction.)

The following poem can be used as an example of moving at different tempos, and as an example of moving lightly.

BLOSSOM

Lightly floating through the air
Blossoms scatter everywhere;

Now the wind begins to mutter,
Blossoms start to twist and flutter,

See them spinning faster now,
See them shaken from the bough!

Now the wind is slowly stopping,
Blossoms to the earth are dropping;

Every white and falling petal
On the ground will softly settle.

The following sequence is suggested:
1) Read the poem
2) Discuss with the children how each verse may best be interpreted in action
3) Speak each verse followed by suitable accompaniment to which the children then move (one verse at a time).

(It's possible for everyone to take the part of falling blossoms, or for some to play the part of the boughs on the tree, swaying heavily about in the wind by contrast.)

Weight

LIGHT AND HEAVY WORDS

Did you know that words could sound light or heavy? First, let's listen to some light and heavy sounds (on the piano, drum, tambourine, or triangle— trills, light taps, thumps, crashes, etc. played as illustrations.)

Now here is a light word, "Flutter." Can you show me how to flutter your hands lightly?

Here is a heavy word, "Lumber." Can you show me how a tractor lumbers along? Bend your knees and make yourself feel all heavy!

Here is another light word, "Whisper." Let's creep about on our toes very softly, saying "Whisper, whisper, whisper." Move in some other very soft, light way now as you keep saying "Whisper" again.

Now here is a heavy word again—"Clang." Let's find a heavy way to move around while we say, "Clang, clang, clang." Let's pretend that we're striking down very hard with a heavy hammer now . . . "Clang, clang, clang!"

More example words to illustrate weight in movement or movement and speech, are as follows:

Light	Heavy
Flicker	Thunder
Flash	Grind
Feather	Stone
Swish	Drag
Slipper	Gong

LIGHT AND HEAVY SONGS

The first line or two of well known nursery rhymes sometimes have a distinctly light or heavy aspect. The words can be spoken with appropriate light or heavy action.

Lines	*Suggested Actions*
Jack be nimble, Jack be quick, Jack jump over the candlestick!	Lightly hopping from foot to foot, pointing alternate index fingers in different directions.
Row, row, row your boat	Effortful rowing action, sitting on the floor. Pulling on an imaginary rope.
Fee Fie Fo Fum	Pushing down with alternate feet into the floor while heavily rocking weight from foot to foot and pushing down clenched fists towards the floor. Lying on back on the floor and pushing body backwards by pressure on alternate feet.
Rock-a-bye Baby On the tree top	Gentle cradling action. Lightly rocking whole body and head from foot to foot.

EARTH, AIR, AND WATER

In this activity, the children are to imagine the different resistances of earth, air, and water as they pretend they are moving through them in turn. Suggestive verbal descriptions and percussion sounds should accompany them. First they can move like a mole or an earthworm pushing through the earth; (heavy action). Then they can stand up and move as if they're swimming the breast stroke through the water; (medium weighted action). Finally, they can imagine they are an eagle soaring in the air; (light action).

Contracting and Expanding

The following poem should be talked about first. Words that are not understood should be explained, such as "trembles" and "shadows" and "shrinks." It may be helpful to bring a candle to class to illustrate the trembling of the candle flame, and how the wax begins to melt. If there is a source of light which will throw suitable shadows (or if one can be contrived) it is most helpful to let the children make shadows with their bodies in different shapes. Children will absorb the words and meaning not only through their minds, when listening, but through their bodies, when moving.

CANDLE

Light the candle in the hall—
Flame trembles, growing tall,
Shadows dance upon the wall.

Up and down the shadows go,
Out and in they shrink and grow—
Round about they twist and flow.

Wax is melting, watch it fall—
Candle shrinks beside the wall'
Flame goes out . . . . . .well is that all?

(It is both interesting and worthwhile to try to experience the complete stillness and emptiness of "being nothing" when the flame has gone out.)

Children are now ready to practice expanding and contracting movements during locomotion (as well as just from a stationary base). The following poem offers an imaginary basis for slowly growing wider, vertically twisting from one side to the other, then slowly growing thinner again, *while walking along.* (Arms slowly raised from sides and extended at shoulder level can depict growing wider. Being "neatly" rolled can be interpreted as a spin on the spot with arms tightly held to sides.)

MRS. WINKLE'S UMBRELLA
I belong to Mrs. Winkle,
When the rain begins to sprinkle
I am opened out —
As she walks about!

Bit by bit I'm opened wider
Till I'm stretched out like a spider,
I begin to twist —
Clutched inside her fist.

Now the rain has finished plopping
Mrs. Winkle's slowly stopping,
Down I start to fold —
Then I'm neatly rolled!

ICE

This is a group project, but it starts and ends in individual space. The children will need to be able to cooperate quite well, and mood music is helpful.

Each child finds a space on his own and imagines that he is a small speck of ice which has formed on a lake. As the weather gets colder and colder each speck of ice grows bigger and bigger. (Children can start in a bunched up crouching position, and gradually rise, extending their arms.)

As the patches of ice grow yet bigger, they start to drift towards each other, and the children join onto each other by holding hands or wrists. They should be in a network rather than in a circle. For example, four children may form one junction, three another, etc. They will need some help to begin with in working out this idea. When a satisfactory network has been formed, the outside children lean outwards and tug gently. The ice cracks in various places as some of the children let go hands (this also provides an exercise in the use of tension). Gradually all the children separate from each other as they lean away and let go. The "pieces" of ice float off so that the children are all on their own again. They may rock back and forth on the water or spin slowly round. They then start to melt by growing smaller and smaller (bunching up more and more into a crouched position again) as they began.

Degree of Tension in the Body

ISOLATION EXERCISE

This is a purely physical exercise which some of the children may find hard to do.

Let's make our legs and feet and arms and hands and back and neck all stiff. We'll stand with our legs apart and make our arms stick out like this. Now we'll keep our legs and feet all stiff, but we'll let our hands go floppy, and our arms go floppy, and our neck go floppy, and our back go floppy - FLOP FLOP FLOP! Can you walk around now with stiff legs and floppy arms and back?

Now reverse this process by starting off with the whole body floppy and then stiffening the upper body while maintaining floppy feet and legs. Children usually find this more difficult, as it's hard to walk with floppy legs.

Isolation exercises of this type in which thought must be brought to bear on different parts of the body in order to "get the message through," greatly aid the development of the body image.

LOOSE OR TIGHT

The children all stand normally, which means neither too stiffly nor too sloppily, and with a good posture. You should then explain that you are going to lightly touch different parts of different children, and that they should then relax or "flop" just that part as much as possible. For example, if you touch someone's head, it will probably just flop forwards. Shoulders, knees, tummies, chests, backs, etc., can all be touched and "flopped".

When children get used to this exercise, they can try it with a partner. One child should do the touching, the other, the flopping. The main point is that the child should attempt to isolate the part that is touched instead of just going generally floppy all over.

Levels

IMAGINARY TUNNEL

Pretend you are moving though an imaginary dark tunnel. Describe it as you go and have the children follow behind you. Mood music is helpful. The aim of this exercise is to move at both low, high, and as many intervening levels as possible. The story can be enhanced by having an imaginary aim in view, which can first be discussed with the children. For example, they could be seeking for hidden treasure, trying to escape from somewhere, or creeping past a monster on the way.

Include: sliding, pushing on your back; wriggling on your tummy; dragging yourself along on your side; crawling on your knees; crouching and moving along in a "duck walk"; walking on hands and feet; groping around—sides, front, above, to see how much space there is; squeezing through a gap backwards; going through very narrow spaces—horizontal, vertical, diagonal; going through occasional caverns in which there is much space and in which you can reach around and stretch out, etc.

OCTOPUS DANCE

It helps to produce a picture of an Octopus and to talk about it first. You can demonstrate how an Octopus reaches out with its arms at different levels, attaching itself to things as it goes (over a rock for example). You can show how it rotates, how it can draw in its arms and then extend them again. You can try to show how it slowly rolls and drops in different positions through the water, and then can slide over the bottom of the sand.

Guided practice of these movements can follow, allowing the

children to experiment further, as they wish, with slow reaching, sliding, turning movements. They should practice exerting different pressures on the walls and floor with the hands and feet as they push and glide. This should be a free slow-motion dance with as much variety of movement as possible through high, medium, and low levels.

Sudden and Sustained Movements

POPCORN—A GROUP GAME UTILIZING SUDDEN MOVEMENT

Let's pretend we're each a small hard piece of corn waiting to be popped in a big pan! Now remember to stay inside the pan because the lid is on and you can't get out!

Here we are all crouching on the bottom of the pan. We're very close to each other in here and nothing seems to be happening. Now someone puts us on the stove and we start to get hot. We feel we want to stretch but we can't because we have a hard coat on. We're getting hotter still—something's going to have to happen because we're pushing so hard against the coat which holds us in . . . . .POP! Our coat splits and we jump right up and hit the lid! We fall down in a heap, but now we're not so small and hard—we're all puffed out and lighter.

Let's do that again. You decide when you're going to pop—it doesn't matter if two or three of you do it at the same time. But try not to go off all together! Off you go! POP POP POP POP POP POP POP! Jump up very suddenly as high as you can.

(You can accompany the children's movement with a sharp tap on the tambourine—*following*—their actions rather than initiating them. The exercise can be repeated but this time the lid is left off the pan so that the popcorn pops right over the edge of the pan and rolls to a standstill . . . the children therefore end up spread out over the room.)

MIST

Twisting gliding mist
Settles on this tree; then lifts
Leaving it trembling.

Interpretive dancing of this haiku involves not only sustained movement but also different levels, light, slow action, and a few seconds of stillness in the middle. The trembling of the tree is a delicate, continuous, vibratory movement in the leaves caused by the stirring of the wind.

These kinds of questions might be put to the children before starting to move:

Can you show me what gliding means?

How can you twist and glide at the same time?

Where do you think the mist comes from?

Does it cover up the whole tree?

What makes the mist go away?

Do you think it all goes at the same time?

Which way does it go?

Can you show us what trembling means?

Who wants to dance the tree?

Who wants to dance the mist?

The children may need help in finding the answers, but the more they contribute through imagining the scene and thinking it out, the more they will be involved in portraying it.

Accompaniment: Vocal sounds by the children, such as a gentle humming or shhhhhhhhh-ing; percussive sounds such as a light tambourine shake or tapping of the triangle (which also could be made by one or two of the children).

It's important not to forget the moment of absolute stillness and silence in the middle of this dance.

Abandoned and Controlled Movements

BLASTING ROCKS

Do you know that sometimes we have to blast rocks out of the way to make a road? Well this is what happens. There is a long thing called a fuse which looks rather like a piece of string. Now the end of the fuse is joined onto some sticks of explosives. These explosives are like very big noisy fireworks which will blow up the rock. The road men light the fuse at one end, and the little flame carefully burns along the fuse . . . like this (little, smooth, hunched over walk with palms together in front of chest).

Now when the tiny flame reaches the end of the fuse, it sets off the sticks of explosive. They blow up and go KABOOM against the rock. The rock all breaks up and jumps into little pieces like this (jumping wildly in crouched position all over the place). *Now how else could the rocks explode?* (The class will usually contribute some graphic illustrations.)

Now let's dance all that. Here's some fuse music (moving carefully in straight line, etc.). *Watch out for the falling rocks, here comes the explosion—KABOOM! BANG BANG BANG BANG BANG,* (etc.).

Motion and Stillness

BEGINNINGS AND ENDINGS

Play the children a short musical tune which slows down slightly as it draws to a close. Ask them to think of how they will dance it, and to imagine a beginning and ending position (same one). Let them listen to the tune about three times (without dancing).

Now ask the children to get into their beginning positions. They should hold these positions for about five seconds before they dance and, at the end, they should hold their chosen positions for another five seconds. When the tune has been danced about three times, most of them will have memorized its length and tried to coordinate their movement to fit.

UNDER THE SEA

In this sequence there are three groups of children:

1) Big, fierce fish that lie under the edge of the coral reef. To begin with they are motionless except for slight fin (hand) movements. Then suddenly, they glide out into the midst of the tiny fish. They sweep about with a rolling motion (this can be done from a moving crouched position).

2) Tiny fish that wiggle and dart, flicking heads and tails (feet). This can be done lying on the floor. When the big, fierce fish come

out from hiding, the tiny ones quickly wriggle away and hide in between pieces of coral.

3) Coral—children form into a still network of arms, backs, and legs, making their stationary position as interesting as possible . . . . . . some on their backs, others on their knees, others sitting or standing, etc. This group remains quite still throughout, despite the surrounding movement and agitation.

The class can be consulted as to what sounds they think would form a suitable percussion background, and then they can help to make them under your direction. After a while, let the children change roles.

The aim of the above game is to foster the ability to stay still while others move.

SEAGULLS

Seagulls on the cliff
Stretch their wings and wait—
Then drift into the wind.

This haiku movement exercise describes movement from a stationary base (stretching) followed by a pause, then sustained movement from a moving base (drifting this way and that). A feeling of expansion while extending the body through chest, arms, and back, should be expressed through the movement.

Active and Passive Movement (Doing and Being Done To)

Now we come to another type of contrast—the degree of being active or passive. Though subtle, this noticeably affects the quality of movement. This idea has already been danced in various ways through the use of imagery. "Passive" movement requires an outside force to motivate it—blossom and falling leaves were moved by the wind and by the force of gravity; the balloon was blown up by a person; seaweed was caused to float about by the sea. "Active" movement is *self* activated. The whirlwind was an active force, (nobody turned it on). Mingus the Monkey as he bounded through the forest and the Caterpillar as it walked around the garden were also in an "active" mode.

Naturally, a child dancing is activating himself. However, the quality of movement differs with the idea portrayed. Active ideas create *assertive* movement and passive ones create movement which is *yielding*—to gravity or other forces. Here are two ways of presenting this concept to four, five, and six year olds—ways which help to reinforce their growing sense of "Hey, I can do it!"

WHO MOVES ME?
I had a mouse I wound with a key,
I ran in a line and it followed me,
But when I zig-zagged on the floor
The mouse went straight just as before!
It couldn't wiggle or jigglety-jiggle
Or run in a circle wild and free!

I had a car I pushed around
In front of me upon the ground,
But left alone it just stayed still
—It couldn't drive itself uphill;
It couldn't wiggle or jigglety-jiggle
Or run in a circle wild and free!

Now do you think I need a key?
Am I stuck or am I free?
You won't see what I'm about
I do it from the inside out—
But when I wiggle and jigglety-jiggle
I'm the one who's moving me!

(Verse 1 and 2 can be enacted with a partner—one child dances the part of "me," the other enacts the parts of the clockwork mouse and the car. Verse 3 can be a free dance.)

CLASS DISCUSSION
Here are some things which start moving by themselves—a chicken coming out of an egg; a cat waking and stretching; a person sweeping leaves; any others? (Class suggestions and movement

practice of examples should follow.)

Here are some things which need to be moved by something or someone else: a snowball being pushed by someone; a leaf being blown by the wind; a twig being carried along by a stream. Any others? (Suggestions and practice again follow.)

The following activities offer further practice in "Doing" and "Being Done To" movements.

THE KITCHEN SHELF

Once upon a time there were a lot of things on the kitchen shelf all having a quarrel. They were arguing about who was the most important.

"I am the most important," said the knife, "because I am strong and straight and can go SLASH SLASH SLASH!"

"No, I am the most important," squeaked the bean, "because I am little and round and can roll around and hide."

"Nonsense," said the rubber band, "no one can stretch like me!"

"And what about me?" asked the plastic bag. "I am so strong that I can hold all of you and yet I am so thin that the light can go right through me."

"I make the light," muttered the flame in the candle, "and I am warm too and can quiver with the air."

How long this would have gone on I do not know, but a voice from below the shelf said, "Hey, wait a minute! I know you all have special gifts, so you can all do some things better than anyone else can. But you can do them only when a person like me makes you do them. Only a person can use a knife, roll a bean, stretch a rubber band, put things in a bag, or light a candle. And a person can do many of the things you can do besides, like rolling and stretching and quivering. Only a person can dance!" And there, jumping up to have a look at the things on the shelf was a person just about as big as you. "Look at me!" she said, and started to dance like this. (Suitable rhythmic accompaniment.)

Knife action . . . . . .Slashing—with as many parts of the body as
                possible

Bean action . . . . . .Rolling—from lying, sitting, kneeling positions.

Rubber Band Action . . . . . .Stretching—in as many directions with as many parts of the body as possible.

Plastic Bag Action . . . . . .Encircling—Have a group of children make a circle around several other children. Let the circle squeeze into the center and spread out again, while the children in the center occupy whatever space is available to them at the time.

Candle action . . . . . .Quiver—with different parts of the body, then with the whole body.

. . . . . .Sway—plus growing up and down.

Well now, after watching all that dancing, the things on the kitchen shelf never boasted about who was the most important again!

THE PUPPET

(See Chapter Seven, "Sensory Contrasts and Combinations," subsection "Degree of Tension in the Body.")

This poem, which was treated in detail in the previous chapter, can be danced with a partner for the first verse. Children can take turns moving their partners into different positions—with gentleness and care! . . . Arms, legs, heads, backs, shoulders, knees, elbows, etc., can all be repositioned. This poem, besides providing the experience of "floppiness," provides a good opportunity to experience the feeling in movement of a passive object becoming self directed.

WODGY WOO

Wodgy Woo is a fictitious character created to illustrate the cause and effect of movement. For the first series of movements, he is the causer of events (which in turn means the child is "being done to" or is passive, in movement response).

Wodgy Woo is blowing a wild wind through the room so that it is difficult to stand up.

Wodgy Woo has taken your hand and is spinning you around.

Wodgy Woo is leaning on you!

Wodgy Woo has put a large, heavy hat on your head!

Wodgy Woo is pushing you backwards into a corner.
(You may need to embellish these statements to make them really effective. For example:) *"Wodgy Woo is tilting the floor up and down. He is making you run downhill first one way and then the other—now sideways, now backwards. It's tilting even more now—is he going to make you fall over?"*

In the second series of events, Wodgy Woo is the one who is "being done to" and the child is the one who is *doing,* or actively causing things.

Now you *are leaning on Wodgy Woo.*

Now you *are spinning Wodgy Woo around.*

Now you *are pushing Wodgy Woo backwards into a corner.*

Now you *are pulling Wodgy Woo along behind you, etc.*

CONDUCTING
In this game, you conduct the way you want the children to move, by pointing and gesturing—back and forth, side to side, up and down, around, slowly, faster, forcefully, limply, briskly, etc.

After finding a partner, the children can take turns conducting each other.

THREE SCARECROWS
*There were three scarecrows in a field
Their arms were straight and thin—o,
They swivelled round upon a stick,
The wind blew out and in—o;
Blow, blow, to and fro,
the wind blew out and in—o.*

*One night there came a sudden storm
The wind roared all around—o;*

One night there came a sudden storm
The wind roared all around —o;
The rain it lashed, the thunder crashed,
The scarecrows fell to the ground —o;
Topple, plop, down they drop,
The scarecrows fell to the ground —o.

When next morning all was calm
A man walked down the field —o;
He saw the scarecrows in a heap
And pulled them up again —o;
Heave and raise in different ways,
He pulled them up again —o.

There are three scarecrows in a field
Leaning all together-o;
When angry storms rush round about
They stand in all the weather —o;
When wind and rain attack again,
They stand in all the weather —o.

An explanation of a scarecrow should be offered, also a picture, if possible. The characters to be danced in this poem are: Scarecrows (Passive); Wind, Rain, Thunder, the Man (Active).

First verse   This can be danced in groups of four—three children being the scarecrows swivelling round on sticks; the fourth being the wind blowing between and around them.

Second Verse   If the class is sufficiently mature, the second verse may be danced around one set of scarecrows with the wind, rain, and thunder portrayers all moving at once while adhering to their respective roles. If the class is likely to get too mixed up with this, *all* the children may play the wind, then the rain, then all play the thunder.

The Wind and (boy) scarecrows

The Wind and (girl) scarecrows

Third Verse   All the children can now play the scarecrows lying on the ground. *You* may play the man in the field who picks them up (they must be limp but cooperative). Lean them together in groups of three in varying positions, so that they support each other and become a strong unit. A couple of volunteers may also play the man in the field, and help you to lean them together.

Fourth Verse   One trio of scarecrows now become wind, and/or rain, and/or thunder. The remaining scarecrows sway about in their leaning groups of three, but they do not yield to the elements, which are doing their worst! The other trios of scarecrows then each take their turn at being the wild weather.

Alternative ways of dancing the poem may well arise and be explored and used.

•Patterns in Space

Body Shape

The following three activities help develop the body image by exploring different ways of forming shapes.

PIPE CLEANER SHAPES WITH A PARTNER

Pipe cleaner shapes can be used as before, but now they can be interpreted not only individually, but with a partner. The ones in the preceding chapter may still be used for solo work, and the series below can be used for partner work. Two children may work out the following shapes with their bodies joined or touching in some way.

Numerous other examples can be discovered.

SLOW MOTION

Ask children to "grow" into any shape they choose and then to continuously keep changing their shape in slow motion. They can begin this idea by copying you. Later, they can do it on their own.

MIRROR GAME

In the last chapter, the children copied you as they pretended to portray your mirror image.

Now the children can play the Mirror Game with a partner. They should take turns leading. It's best if *you* tell them which one of them is to begin, and after a while to stop the activity and ask the other partner to take over, otherwise precious time is often taken up as they argue who is to start. Ask them to keep their movement slow and big, to keep facing each other, and to stay in the same spot. (Later on they might try moving very slowly across the floor if they feel like it, but at first they have enough to think about without adding locomotor movement.) It's best if you precede the exercise with a demonstration with another person.

Changing shape in slow motion

Mirror game

Floor Patterns

MOVING OUTWARDS FROM A FOCAL POINT AND BACK TOWARDS
IT AGAIN

There are many ways of moving outwards from a center in space and back towards it again. The three below are useful in developing space awareness for this age group.

The middle of the room can serve as the center and you can create a focal point by standing there. Gather the children around you and draw this diagram for them:

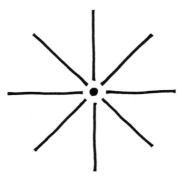

Ask the children if they can each move like one of the lines leading away from you, backwards to the edge of the room. Then get them to return along the same route. After the exercise, talk about what happened, asking those children who did it correctly to demonstrate to the rest. Then get the class to attempt the task once more.

The following three diagrams give harder alternatives:

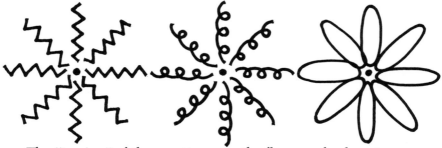

The "tracing" of these patterns on the floor can be done in many ways. Here are some suggestions:

Method of locomotion:　skipping; hopping; galloping; wriggling; sliding; crawling; jumping

Directions: —forwards; backwards; sideways
Sensory contrasts: —fast/slow; light/heavy; high/low; stiff/floppy;
    sudden/sustained, etc.

Directions

FISHING FLOAT

Constantly changing level and direction characterize this exercise. Doing two things at once, such as moving upwards and
sideways, is now within the children's grasp whereas a year ago they
would probably have been confused by the attempt. Describe the
waves of the sea and how the float is being moved by them. The
child responds by moving up and down, forwards, sideways,
diagonally, and around. You might say:

*Here comes a big wave. The float goes up, up, up, and moves
sideways too, like this . . . Now the wave goes down again and the
float goes down, down, down. Here in between the waves the float
goes down a little bit more, turning around at the same time. Here
comes a little wave and the float just bobs up a bit, going forwards,
and then down a bit, going backwards, (etc.).*

You will find that at first you will need to demonstrate as you
speak. Later, it may be possible to give directions with the voice
only.

This exercise can also be done in a group by getting the children
to hold hands in a circle, as if the individual floats were now on the
periphery of a net. The children should try to keep holding hands
(not to break the circle by moving too vigorously) and should be
flexible enough to let their circle assume a changing shape, like an
amoeba, as they flow back and forth, up and down, and from side to
side. They can try going around both far apart and close together.

As, in this information, some children will be going backwards
while others go forwards and sideways, you can direct the pro-
ceedings by asking individual children to take a turn leading the
circle backwards.

Here is another fun way of practicing different levels and directions.

FALLING

Blow blow swishy breeze
Brush the leaves off the trees;
This way, that way, make them blow,
Round in circles make them go . . .
Blow me, blow me off the tree—
This is my way, look at me!
Now we roll into a heap—
Now we lie in winter sleep.

Suggested approach to interpretation

Guided practice: 1) ask children to describe in the air how a leaf falls to the ground, with hand and arm movements.

2) Practice "swishy" breeze blowing "this way" and "that way" . . . each child holds a scarf and wields it in a flowing, sweeping manner all around the room, high and low. Tambourine shake and beat provide suitable accompaniment. (The shake indicates sweeping action, the beat is a signal to change level and/or direction.)

3) Arrange the children into groups of three (back to back) to form the trunk and branches of a tree. Practice swaying with the wind—bodies swaying gently in unison, while all six arms slowly wave in different directions to intermittent tambourine shake.

4) Discover as many ways as possible of interpreting "round in circles" (i.e., not only moving from different basic positions at different levels, but also facing sideways, backwards, and forwards in the chosen circle, plus leading with different parts of the body). The circles may be made by pivoting on the spot, by rotating while moving across the floor, or by tracing circles on the floor. If the class has difficulty in tracing imaginary circles, it helps to have them move around the outside of a hoop first. Then remove the hoop and ask them to imagine it while going around.

5) You can now "conduct" the leaves as in the section on "conducting" (see the section on Sensory Contrasts and Combinations, subheading "Active and Passive Movement" occuring earlier in this chapter). This will give the children practice in moving in ways they may not yet have discovered for themselves in this exercise.

Free interpretation of the poem can now follow, to suitable mood music if possible. Three volunteers form the tree and the rest can join on as leaves. They are then blown free of the tree (aided by percussion sounds) and drift, swirl, glide, and spin about and around, finally sinking in different ways and rolling (as if they were being blown) into a heap where they then lie quite still. (The tree can go on swaying and bending until the end, when it too becomes quite still.)

If this poem works out well, you can vary it by asking the children to make a special leaf shape which they try to approximate throughout the dance.

Little Way and Long Way

ROCKET

Now pretend you are going to move like a little Halloween rocket. Someone is lighting you and you swoosh up in the air a little way, and then you burn out and drop down.

Now you are like a very big fireworks rocket. You are going to Swoosh in just the same way, but this time you will go much further—right to the side of the room. Are you ready? SWOOOOOOOOOOOOOOOOOSH! Now you burn out and drop quietly to the floor.

POINT AND TURN ABOUT

It's possible to do this activity without any accompaniment. Each child faces in any direction, pointing in front of himself. He goes in the direction of his finger for a *little way*, stops, turns and retraces his steps. Then he stands still. After a second he jumps, turning to another direction, and goes through the same procedure, but this time he goes a *long way* before returning.

HOW CLOSE

Yet another way of expressing the idea of a little way and a long way is by actually bringing different parts of the body close to one another, and then move them as far away from each other as possible. For example, two hands; two feet; a hand and a foot; head and a knee; elbow and back; wrist and tummy; heel and seat, etc.

This can also be done *with a partner*. Each child should be close to his partner on a stationary base. For example, both children could be sitting down close to each other, and then they bring their heads very close. Then they lean away backwards so that their heads are as far away from each other as possible, while still keeping their seat in the same position. Another example might be two children kneeling back to back, bringing their backs very close or touching, then lying on their tummies while they make their backs as far away as possible, without moving their knees. It's good to experiment with different basic positions in this game.

Our Own Space

Children of this age are better able to maintain their own space. Many activities and stories may be begun by suggesting that they go and find a space to themselves where no one is near to them. Encourage them to move into the corners of the room, which are often neglected.

•Props

All suggestions in the previous chapter are equally useful for this stage. While props are still most *desirable* for creating concrete working aids, and while they are just as stimulating and fun to work with, they gradually become less *necessary*. The exception is in the area of space exploration, where diagrams and pictures are essential to carrying out certain ideas. The reason for this is that the child is now able to work more directly from imagination. Sensory experience of the world, memory and concentration are now useable tools.

•Dancing with a Partner

Many partner activities now occur in the context of what is going on. There is a marked improvement in cooperation, and children greatly seem to enjoy working out movements and ideas together. They seem to find it emotionally enriching.

UNDER AND OVER

Can you use your own body in some way to make a tunnel for your partner to crawl through? Well, now make yourself into a shape that your partner can step over. Use your legs, arms, back, and tummy for making these shapes. Keep changing around with your partner—make shapes for each other to crawl under or step over, and be careful not to jump on each other!

•Listening

All "listening" suggestions and comments in the previous chapter are appropriate for this age group.

General training of listening response will depend largely on your attitude. When musical accompaniment is being used, any chattering will blur receptivity. Rhythm, mood, and tempo are best heard clearly rather than vaguely apprehended through a blanket of voices.

Some educators feel that children can learn best when allowed to chatter freely; however, in the area of movement, children learn best when they are allowed to *listen*. In some partner and group activities talking is necessary for the working out of ideas, but within the dance itself random speech seems to detract from the intensity of movement expression.

Generally speaking, a minimal degree of chatter and a high degree of listening involvement can be achieved without too much difficulty as long as you yourself convey a listening attitude, and bring back the attention of the class when necessary. Listening then becomes a positive activity rather than the repression of speech.

Sometimes one or two children in a class are very bad listeners, and this can destroy the concentration for everybody. If a child is poor at listening, and if he has no hearing defect, he has quite possibly never been expected to listen very much and is used to making an unlimited amount of noise. Interestingly, these children often behave "out of context" and will break across the most exciting part of a story with some unrelated idea, "I've got two grandpas and one grandma" or "Guess what—I had a banana for breakfast!" Another thing they might do is to talk very loudly to another child when everyone is lying quietly and listening to the music. Through their inability to listen they genuinely seem to be out of touch with what is going on around them. It takes time and patience to help them to

Tunnels (Under and over game)

be aware through their ears, and it's necessary to bring their attention back continually, reengaging their interest. Although these attempts are sometimes frustrating, progress can definitely be made, and within a few months such children sometimes become good listeners.

USING MUSICAL FORM AS A BASIS FOR LISTENING AND DOING

The first musical form to be used should be A B (i.e., there are two distinct sections to the piece). One section might be faster or in a different rhythm or key. Half the class should dance A and the other half, B. The piece should be repeated and danced several times while the children try to identify "their" dance. Once this can be done easily, a more complex form can be introduced—A B C, (a piece of music with *three* distinct sections).

When the children are familiar with the music of A B C, half the class can dance A, and half, B, as before. *All* the class can dance to the C section. This will be quite a challenge!

•Concentrating on the Movement

At around five years old, children seem to direct their attention into the movement more consciously, giving it a quality of definition and individuality. The following two exercises are designed to promote this quality of being focused in action. The author has found that once the child has experienced the enriching feeling which concentration brings, he will try to reproduce it whenever he can.

WATCHING MY HAND

Standing up, hold one hand in front of you. Look at the finger tips. Look hard at the finger tips and don't look anywhere else. Now start to move a bit with your feet, across the floor, as you move your hand around. Keep your eyes just watching the top of your fingers all the time. Gently move your hand up, down, and from side to side. Out of the corner of your eye you'll see the rest of the room, but you don't have to think about it. You'll be able to tell if you're going to bump into anything. Just keep watching your fingers.

After the children have been trying this out in the space of the whole room, it's helpful to ask them to come into a circle. Then ask one or two children who have succeeded well in this exercise to demonstrate in the middle of the circle. After that, ask for volunteers. The standard of ability will have gone up considerably just through having watched others. In a few minutes most chidren will have developed the art of moving and keeping their eyes and minds on the tips of their fingers, although some will move more freely and with a more extended range of action.

They can now do this exercise watching both hands, then watching a knee and then watching a foot. (This might mean they are down close to the floor.)

The next, and hardest, stage is to ask the children to *pretend* they are watching their backs, heads, sides, hands, etc. and to think about the place that is chosen very hard all the time, so that they have a picture of it inside their heads, while they are dancing. It doesn't matter that this process is hard to assess. Rest assured that any level of success strengthens the mind-body connection.

MOVING ON THE BREATH

Certain movements acquire much more of a centered quality when performed on a deep inhalation or exhalation of the breath. Perhaps this is because the way we breathe and the way we feel are so intimately related. In order for the children to monitor their breathing properly it's necessary when doing these movements to breathe audibly. The best way of doing this is to inhale and exhale to specific sounds. The following are suggested sounds, and their appropriateness will depend on the type of movement needed.

*Breathing out:*Shhhhhhhhh; Hoo Hoo Hoo; Ffffffffff; Haaaaaaaaaaaaa.

Breathing in: (Lips pursed) Fffffffff; Uuh Uuh Uuh; Aaaaaaaaaaaaa.

The following are suggested movements:

1) *Exhale*....Rise upwards from a crouched position and stretch to the "sky" while *inhaling.* Sink and curl downwards while *exhaling.*

2) *Inhale*....Spin none way while *exhaling. Inhale* again.....Spin the

other way while *exhaling*. (N.B. —when the breath starts to run out, the spinning should get slower until both stop together.)

3) *Inhale*....With hands raised above head in a clenched fist position, stamp first one foot and then the other with aggressive downward thrusting action of the fists and short sharp outbursts of exhaled breath.

4) *Inhale*....Stagger and droop to one side while *exhaling*. Quickly *inhale* while straightening. Repeat on the other side.

N.B. It's well known, of course, that some of the Martial Arts utilize voiced exhalations which seem to gather the energy together.

The following movement story contains examples of moving on the breath.

WHISPER

Once upon a time there was a whisper waiting to be whispered by someone. It SSSSSSSSd, swaying around all over the place, wanting someone to find it. But no one did. So it got sad and droopy and signed just like this, Pffffffff! Then it lifted itself up to look around again. As it lifted itself up it said, Uuuuuuuuuuuuuuuh! But no one was there and it shrank down again - Pfffffffff!

Just then a big wind came and blew the whisper right up into the air above the treetops. The whisper was tossed round and round, high in the air. It sounded like this through the trees, "Shhhhhhhh, shhhhhhhhh, shhhhhhh," as their heavy branches swayed around. It sounded like this around the chimney, "Whoooooooo, whoooooooooo, whoooooooooo!" Then it dropped straight on top of the little flickering flames in the fireplace below, that went like this, "Sw sw sw sw sw sw sw sw sw." It floated right out into the room on the smoke, holding its breath.

Just then it got up someone's nose. "Achooooo! Achooooo! Achooooo!" And it hopped about in little explosions.

At that point Dad caught the whisper as he stretched and yawned like this "Uuuuuuuuuuuuuuuuuu—Haaaaaaaaaaaaaa aaaaa!" Then Mom said, "time for bed!" The children were the next to catch the whisper as they groaned, "Huuuuuuuuuuuur!" But they were tired just the same and the whisper crept into bed with them where it was quiet and warm.

In the middle of the night, the whisper could be heard in the sound of the children's breathing, "Aahaa aahaa aahaa aahaa." That's a comfortable sound isn't it? And the whisper wasn't lonely any more.

•Action Words as Stimuli for Movement

Children between four and a half and six years old have a much wider command of words than they had a year ago. It's now possible to use a single word to express the essence of an action.

These single words can be grouped under collective headings or used at random. For this age group, collective headings have been taken from the world around us, as follows:

The Weather:
Snow—twists   drifts   drops
Wind—rushes   whirls   swishes
Fog—spreads   glides   rises
Rain—patters   slashes

Animals:
A lion—prowls   springs   paces
A tortoise—shuffles   drags   waits
A rabbit—jumps   scuffles   freezes
A bird—floats   sinks   rises

Methods of Locomotion:
A truck—zooms   reverses
A plane—glides   banks   swoops
A boat—sways   dips   drifts   rocks

Toys:
Playdough—sqeezes   stretches
Blocks—balance   collapse
A Ball—bounces   rolls   stops
A swing—swings   twists

Under the Sea:
Sea anemone—uncurls   waves   curls
Seaweed—rises   sinks   bobs   stretches
A fish—wiggles   darts   rolls (from side to side)
Sand—trembles   sinks

At the Circus:
A Clown—staggers   falls   rocks
A tightrope walker—balances   tips
An elephant—sways   swings

These words, and similar action words, can now be presented in "The Envelope Game."

THE ENVELOPE GAME

The Grab Bag approach creates a more effective focus of interest for preschoolers than a straightforward presentation of the words would. The idea is to produce an envelope with different action words written on separate slips of paper contained within it. Ask a child to pull out a slip of paper and read the action word on it, explaining the meaning if necessary. Everybody then tries to interpret the word. Guided practice may be necessary.

Children are eager to "have their turn" in pulling out a word and many kinds of movement can be dealt with in this way. Four or five words are probably enough to cope with in one week.

Demonstration of the interpretations offered followed by discussion and augmentation where necessary, are valuable ways of learning.

•More Stories, Poems, and Games

This story lends itself to all kinds of additions. So long as the ideas have good movement value, the story can incorporate various strange creatures and circumstances.

TRIP TO PLANET X

Everybody spread out and find a space of your own. Now we are going to move as if we were rockets! Find a position crouched down, near to the floor, and be ready to spring up. I'm going to count like this — 5, 4, 3, 2, 1, Zero! and when I say "zero" I shall crash the gong like this! Then you can go zooming out into space making the shape of a rocket with your hands and body—make sure you don't knock anyone over! When I make a clattering sound with the gong on the floor (or some other appropriate sound) like this, that will be the signal for your crash-landing. When you land on the floor, part of you should be lying on the ground of Planet X, and the rest of you should be sticking up into the air. See if you can make yourself into an interesting shape when you land. We'll have a practice first, then we'll do it again properly. Ready for the countdown?

Suggested Actions and Encounters after crash-landing:

Space Walk—Slow-motion undulating movement

Lizards of Jelly Lake—Dragging along the floor on front, side, and back, with one body part at a time sticking above the surface of the lake (leg, arm, head, seat, knee, shoulder, tummy, etc.)

Wild Wonky Woos—Slow creeping motion as Wonky Woos leave their earthdome, followed by wild abandoned dance covering much space and using all parts of the body, ending with slow creeping motion back to their earthdome again.

Black Bats—Upside down (head lower than knees) standing position with arms up above head behind shoulders, as if holding branch. Sideways rocking "walk" along branch in this upside down position. "Flying" with head still down (looking up), darting first in one direction then in another.

One-footed Giants—Large, heavy movements using one foot only in contact with the floor. The giant should move through the basic positions with one foot (lying, kneeling, sitting, all fours, standing, etc.) Repeat with other foot.

Blind Quatrapus—Slow motion on all fours with eyes closed. Rolling over and reaching, groping motions of hands and feet.

The Blips—These creatures move in quick staccato fashion—then suddenly stop and freeze. After a while they move in the same way again. This can be done in silence, while the children choose their own timing.

After escaping from each of these creatures in turn, the space travellers return (space walk again) to find the rocket, only to discover that it has been taken away, and a Flying Saucer put in its

Lizards of Jelly Lake

Blind quatrapus

place! Another countdown is given. On "Zero" everyone both spins and moves along at the same time, finishing up with another crash-landing on Earth!

It may seem at first glance that the following poem would be too difficult to comprehend for preschoolers. However, it worked very successfully with a group of five and six year olds who had been doing creative dance for nearly a year. The poem was first read, quietly and slowly. Then we had a short discussion to make sure that the children understood both the separate words and the composite word pictures. The poem was then read again. Three of the children were clearly inspired by the sense of poetry and they carried this feeling over into their dancing, as their eyes glowed and their movements reflected sensitive awareness.

SNOW

Snow comes from the north;
A little chill wind rises and falls and tells me it is coming.
First one flake
Then another and another
Drift, twist, slowly to the earth.
Then all at once it seems
The sky is dancing down
In little light pieces —
The whole world is flickering white . . . .
I close my eyes; darkness, stillness.
Only the little chill wind rises and falls.

Suggestions for the dance:
1) Move as the wind does—rising and falling to Shhhhhhh and Aaaaaaaaaah, on the breath.
2) Move as the snow does. Point first to one child, then another, then another, until they are all doing the snowflake dance. The following words can be explored (some are in the poem and others are additional); all are suitable for snow movements: Drifting, twisting, gliding, flickering, jiggling, darting, floating, creeping, etc. The children can try to go through the spaces in between each other, so that they are weaving in and out, to whatever snow action they choose.

3) Snow stopping movements: Gradual sinking, dropping, and freezing. Then, as the snow blows lightly over the ground, gentle rolling, rocking, waving movements. Maybe the snow can blow into a big drift.
4) On a stationary base with eyes closed, sway, rise, and fall, vocalizing the sound of the wind again.
5) The dance can end with three soft thuds on the drum, and complete stillness.

This dance can be performed by reading a line or two of the poem at a time (after the initial reading) and dancing each section to vocalization, as suggested, and perhaps with a little percussion here and there to give a sense of rhythm and drama.

The action in the following poem can be interpreted as both you and the class think fit. Bear in mind that almost all the actions can be done either standing up or in some position on the floor. Using as many parts of the body as possible, and as many levels and directions as possible, there is a lot of scope for expression. As usual, it's best to read one idea at a time.

In order to allay any potential fears of the crocodile (after all, being eaten is a pretty basic terror) make sure to depict him as rather a stupid fellow who cannot possibly catch the children, because they are much too clever for him!

THE CROCODILE

I stood on the banks of the River Nile
Smiling at a Crocodile.
It said, "A person served on toast
Is just the food I love the most."
I said, "I will not be your dinner,
I'm much too thin, and growing thinner!"
So I grew as thin as thin as I could
Till the Crocodile said, "Well that's no good—
I'll pour you from my gravy boat!"
"Oh no, I'll jump around in your throat!"
So I jumped around as best I could
Till the Crocodile said, "Well that's no good—
I'll cook you up inside my pot!"
"Oh no—I'll be a stringy knot!"

So I knotted up as best I could
Till the Crocodile said, "Well that's no good—
I'll bake you up inside my pie!"
"Oh no—I'll wriggle around like a fly!"
So I wriggled and jiggled as best I could
Till the Crocodile said, "Well that's no good—
I think I'll put you in my stew!"
"Oh no—I'll kick inside of you!"
So I kicked and punched as best I could
Till the Crocodile said, "Well that's no good—
I'll make you into my dessert!"
"Oh no—I'm sharp and I would hurt!"
So I grew as sharp as sharp as I could
Till the Crocodile said, "Well that's no good—
I'll swallow you in my inside!"
"Oh no, I'm really much too wide!"
So I grew as wide as wide as I could
Till the Crocodile said, "Well that's no good—
You're much too clever for me today....
I think you'll have to go away!"
So I climbed out of the River Nile—
And waved "goodbye" to the Crocodile!

MORE HAIKUS FOR DANCING

Here are four more haikus for dancing, which are suitable for five and six year olds. It's important once more to make sure that the word pictures are understood. Discussing them first with the children and asking them for *their* ideas often results in a variety of interesting suggestions for interpretation which must then be coordinated. Sometimes, at least three different interpretations emerge, which can be danced separately. The first two haikus both contain sudden and sustained motion, falling, and a sense of largeness and heaviness.

THE FALLING TREE
Chop! The tree shudders—
A slow lean, a sudden twist—
It splits and crashes!

The following haiku can be enacted either singly, or else in a long line, with children holding hands as the wave rises, then separating from each other as it foams and crashes:

THE BREAKING WAVE

The slow wave rises,
Curls and bursts with bubbling foam —
And then the great crash!

The next two haikus both contain fast action, then slower action, and a light, drifting quality.

"Dust" involves random grouping, changing into formation grouping, while continuous movement takes place.

DUST

Spinning specks of dust
Gather in a drifting stream
And float through the door.

The next haiku could be done in three or four small groups or else in one big group.

SMOKE

The leaping flames sink,
And out of the sighing wood
Drifts one thread of smoke.

The following movement poem/game involves moving with the eyes closed towards a source of sound. It's inevitable that some of the children "peek" from time to time, but as long as most of them have their eyes closed most of the time, it doesn't matter. The word "lair" usually needs to be explained.

THE GIANT'S LAIR

My friend was jumping on the hill,
And then he wasn't there —
He'd fallen through a special trap
Above a giant's lair!

Suggested Action: Jumping, leaping, collapsing

Flames

I crept across to where my friend
Had vanished through the hole;
Then all at once I fell down too,
And I began to roll.

Creeping, collapsing, rolling, with eyes closed.

I heard a most tremendous snore
And found I could not see
—I felt around to find my friend
So we might both get free.

Groping about to find another child, with eyes closed. Help may be needed. Gong or drum can indicate area of snoring giant, which should be avoided.

At last we met, and holding hands
We tried to get outside;
We let the singing birds out there
Become our special guide.

Holding hands and wriggling in some position on the floor towards direction of tinkling sound being made at other end of room (percussion).

We didn't dare go near the giant
Who went on snoring still;
At last we found a rabbit hole
Which led us from the hill.

At some point request that one child in the partnership holds the ankle of his partner, instead of his hand. The two children now move in a straight line down the rabbit hole, instead of side by side.

And when we slithered up the hole
And climbed into the air,
We ran away and never more
Played round the giant's lair.

Some marker can indicate when the children have reached the open air—either a chalk line drawn across the end of the room, a line of skipping ropes tied together, or a row of chairs which must be passed between. When they have passed this they can open their eyes, let go of each other, and stand up.

N.B. Child helpers can play the percussion as needed, as you will be needed to assist here and there.

WITHOUT (A GAME)

Once children have developed a fairly comprehensive body image, they can learn to dance *without* moving certain parts of their bodies. This helps them to get the maximum use of what is left.

Without Feet can be done either standing with feet wide apart for balance and remaining sqarely on the floor while trying to discover as many ways of moving from this position as possible (as in "Mr. Hoppity and the Shoes"); or else it can be done in constantly changing floor positions while keeping both feet continuously off the floor.

Without One Foot involves balance and the child should be encouraged to move from a floor position to a standing position and back again, as well as moving while staying mainly in contact with the floor (with one foot in the air). Hopping on one foot can be practiced also, as well as standing on one foot and moving the body into different balance positions. (Children usually find this kind of balancing difficult to do.)

Without Arms and Hands can be done in a variety of ways, but those movements which would normally require balance, such as bending, swaying, spinning, rising, or sinking, should be attempted. Arms can be crossed on the chest, held by the sides, or hands held behind the back.

Without One Arm and Hand is an interesting practice in counter-balance.

Without Eyes—Movements on the floor, such as rolling, dragging, or rocking, can be done safely in a group with eyes closed. If children accidentally "bump" they will be moving sufficiently slowly not to hurt themselves. This exercise trains children to sense the space and objects around them. As they have few outside distractions, they

Without one foot

then become more acutely aware of the way they are moving. It's a good idea to warn children not to move with their eyes closed when they have no one to watch where they are going, particularly if they are dancing with their eyes closed while standing up.

DANCING TO THE FOUR CORNERS (A GAME)

The Following activity repeats the idea used in "The Giant's Lair"—moving towards a source of sound with the eyes closed.

Four children, holding one percussion instrument apiece, sit just a little way in from the four corners of the room. Under your direction, they play their instruments in turn. Point to the child who is to play, and when you want him to stop, raise your hand in a suitable gesture. Then point to another child to play, etc.

In the middle of the room a child stands with his eyes closed. When one instrument sounds, he dances towards the sound. He must stop as soon as it ceases, and then move towards the next instrument sound source. If he is going to fall or bump himself, immediately say "stop!"

It's best to demonstrate the idea first yourself, and then to ask for volunteers. Children can also take turns playing the different instruments.

Generally, children very much enjoy the feeling of dancing with their eyes closed, but a few are always rather timid about it at first. For this reason it's best to tell them that they can open their eyes any time they really feel they want to. Those children who can dance the most easily with their eyes closed generally have the greatest confidence and fluency of movement when they have their eyes open.

•Dividing the Material into Lessons

The same basic attitude should prevail as in previous chapters, namely, that the lesson plan should be a flexible guide, and that a comprehensive background to movement should be developed over the weeks. Each class should contain circle activities, rhythm development, a story or poem, space exploration and/or sensory contrast practice. Movement themes can be worked on for a longer period of time within the lesson than with younger age-groups, and so the potpourri method gradually emerges into a more logical framework.

Three quarters of an hour is still a good lesson length, although an hour is also satisfactory. Not all groups can hold out for an hour. Others can easily cope.

There is enough material in this chapter (in combination with relevant activities from the preceding chapter) for about eighteen months.

CHAPTER NINE

OUTDOOR CREATIVE MOVEMENT

One of the frequent problems besetting a preschool teacher or day-care supervisor who wants to do dancing with the children in her care, is lack of a suitable indoor space. All is not lost, however. Many movement activities readily translate into an outdoor setting. A garden, a neighboring park, a beach, or a field—all can offer a wonderful area to dance in, when the weather is agreeable.

When I was teaching Early Childhood Education students at Camosun College, Victoria, the course I devised was based on the material which now comprises this book. One of my main objectives in teaching the course was to enable each student to improvise confidently and to build imaginatively on the principles and ideas given. It's impossible to teach Creative Dance by rote as the children need to have a spontaneous and adaptable instructor.

This was one of the assignments given to the students towards the end of their course: "Write down a series of activities, in appropriate sequence, suitable for doing out-of-doors for half an hour on a fine day. Define the outdoor area you have in mind: e.g., a field; a concrete playground with grass and trees at one end; a beach, etc. Try to make the activities link up with the outside environment—the weather, nature objects, what can be seen and heard and felt and smelled. Give enough detail so that someone could teach from your outline, even with no background in the subject."

The following selection of excerpts from their responses is from about half the students in one of these classes, and provides wonderful and thoughtful examples of what can be done outdoors.

THE BEACH:

ANNE GRAHAM

Let's sit in a circle and look at the things around us. Look up at the sky. What's in the sky? Clouds? Sun? Birds? Let's watch the birds. What are they doing? Watch how they soar in the sky, flying without flapping their wings. Watch how they dive straight down, trying to catch a fish for their dinner.

Let's pretend we are seagulls. Flap your arms and then soar, keeping your wings straight out. Now let's try to catch some dinner. Look down at the water. Can you see any fish jumping? Let's dive down and catch one. Did you catch one? Good! Now let's fly up to the cliffs. See them, way up there? We can eat our fish up there. Have you ever seen how a seagull eats a fish? He holds it under one claw like this and then eats it with his beak. Let's pretend to eat our fish this way.

Now for desert. What do you think a seagull would like for dessert? How about a clam? Let's fly around again and look for clams. When you spot one, dive down and pick it up in your beak. Do you know how a seagull opens a clam shell? He flies way up high with the clam in his beak and then drops it on some rocks. The clam will break open. Let's fly way up and drop our clams on some rocks. Now fly down and eat your dessert.

WENDY SANFORD

Now feel the ground. Is it soft? Is it hard? Is it sand, gravel, or what? Close your eyes and feel it. Open your eyes. Is it windy today? Carefully pick up some sand and drop it. Be careful it doesn't get in your eyes. Let's all stand up and be sand blowing in the wind, all around the beach, and when I clap my tambourine you can fall to the ground?

Point out the rhythm of the waves. Listen to it briefly. Sound the rhythm out with hands, voices, or with sticks and/or rocks from the beach. Move different parts of the body to the rhythm—ask the children for suggestions.

ANGELA COVIL
Have the children draw designs in the sand with different parts of their bodies. The designs could be used to represent the basic lines from actual objects on the beach. (Some interpretations might be a kite, a rock, seaweed, or a piece of driftwood.) Then they could imitate the shape of the designs with their bodies.

TERESA DAVISON
You can try running along the shore, then jumping. Does the sand feel different under your shoes than it does between your toes? (The children get a different sensation of the sand as they walk around slowly.)

"ROWBOAT"—GERDA STANBRIDGE
—*Let's all put on our lifejackets.*
—*Step into rowboat and sit down.*
—*Pick up oars and row slowly.*
—*Gentle breeze becomes stronger.*
—*Row faster.*
—*Storm comes up, row faster.*
—*Boat bounces up and down, side to side.*
—*Wind dies down, row slowly.*
—*Wind picks up again, row faster.*
—*Boat bounces again, up and down, side to side.*
—*Row fast back to shore.*
—*Jump out of boat, pull rope and swim to shore.*
—*Crawl up to beach, rest, stand up and shake off!*

TRACY TRUSCOTT
Find a distinguishing mark (large rock, log, etc.) a short distance down the beach. Tell the children to fly like sea birds to the mark and back again. The children will most likely enjoy this active, free movement, so let them do it for a few minutes. Call the birds back to the nest (circle), when you feel they've had enough. Ask the children to lie down on their backs and relax.

They may close their eyes or open them if they wish. Talk soothingly to the children. Describe the waves gently rolling, the wind skimming across the water, or anything that is calming and relaxing. Go to each child and gently pick up a leg or arm, or the upper torso, to see if the child is relaxed. Do this with each child, until they are all feeling relaxed. Ask them if they can feel the warm sun and the breeze. This is a good relaxation exercise, especially after an energetic activity; it will quieten the children down and recharge them. When they are sufficiently relaxed, ask them to slowly sit up.

A FIELD:

CHRIS COTÉ

Talk about the grass you are sitting in, and the soil underneath it. Ask the children what kind of animals might be living in the soil or in the grass. Have them try to become the animals they suggest. (Examples: Beetle, worm, grasshopper, snake).

LOUISE CAMPSALL

Hand out one medium size paper bag to each child (name on bag). Instruct the children to search for nature items on the ground. (Remind them not to break off any flowers or buds still attached to plants.) Draw ideas from them: "Can you think of some things you might look for? This is a time to bend down very low and look very carefully." Remain an overseer—encourage self discovery. Guide those who feel unsure. Promote cooperation through helping each other. Give them a couple of minutes. When you're sure all the chldren have at least a couple of items, ask them to run as fast as they can to you. Now you and the children can share your discoveries.

Ask the children to take an object from their bags and to examine it closely, running their finger tips over its surface. Now ask them to find a space by themselves, and using the ground, air, or both, grow into the shape of the nature object. Emphasize the slow gradual growth. Guide individual children where necessary. "I saw some very interesting shapes...Michael show us your shape." Remind Michael to show the beginning, middle, and end of the movement. "Great Michael!...Let's see all of you grow into the shape of a bent twig like Michael. Remember, change your shape very slowly." Make variations known to the children. Help them to see other possibilities. "You made a shape on the ground, now can you make that shape on your knees, or the side of your body?" Finish with everyone finding a partner and making a shape together.

WENDY WESTOBY

Next all lie down on the grass on your backs and silently watch the clouds, the trees swaying, being aware of all the sounds and smells, colors and shapes. (Then ask the children what they saw and what qualities the things around them have, and then move to them. Assuming it is a nice day in a field, the movements will probably be rather gentle, flowing, controlled, such as flowers growing, a breeze, grass blowing; then strike the tambourine because a "storm" has just hit! Play quick, sharp rhythms and have the children dance as if all the things they saw and felt were in a storm.)

MARGARET HOYT

Now does anyone know the name of that big tree? (Then one boy said "an acorn" and picked one up.) *Yes, that is from that Oak Tree. Pass the acorn around so we can all see and feel it. Now let us stand up and very quietly make a big circle around the tree. First feel the tree and see how rough the bark is. What a lovely circle. Now drop your hands and curl up on the ground like an acorn. An acorn is the seed of the Oak Tree. Now begin to grow very slowly. Good, now stretch, stretch, and stretch. Good, keep stretching your arms, now your wrists and fingers. Good stretching! Open your fingers and stretch just like the tree. Now relax your arms and gently sway in the breeze raising your arms as branches. Now the wind gets stronger; move as in a strong wind.* (Use a tambourine for movement control.) *Move with the wind, but no further away than the biggest branch!*

SUSAN OTIS

Talk about the wind—the sounds it makes. (Increase vocabulary.) *Can you see it?*

VALERIE HALA

Let's pretend we are a little dandelion seed. A breeze comes along and blows us all over—we float—up and down, sideways, around and around, lightly, slowly, we fall to the ground.

BEACON HILL PARK, after observing Peacocks and Swans

LINDA MCCUAIG

Let's stand and stretch now. Let's be Peacocks. Let's spread, spread our feathers. (Knees bent, hands behind back, gradually bring arms out in a semi-circle arc.) *Now all the blue peacocks go for a walk* (single out the children wearing blue). *Now all the green peacocks go for a walk* (single out the children wearing green). *Now all the peacocks of every other color go for a walk.* (Have the children wind about in single file, train fashion; imitate the peacock's haughty walk, head held high, wings outspread.)

(Have the children rest now—have them curl up in balls.)

Let's be swans now, sleepy, sleepy swans. Stretch out on your tummies and close your eyes. Pretend you are floating, floating, on the water . . . . . .let's listen carefully, let's be very very quiet. (Let there be absolute quietness for a few seconds while the children rest and relax.)

Now wake up swans, wake up! Gently stretch your long necks....

EPILOGUE

This book has been an attempt to clarify a process which is often spontaneous. The state of mind which enables our actions to promote growth and generate awareness is so bound up with the flux of the moment that it is hard to analyze. The bond between the teacher and the taught, and the dancer and the dance, is at once intimate and tenuous, ever changing, ever bonding, and always new.

It is hoped that this sense of flow has not been lost in pinning down the why's and wherefore's and technical format for teaching. It is hoped that the dancing spirit of the child has prevailed through all the rhyme and the reason.

> *Is it chance or dance that moves the world?*
> *Is the world blind and dumb or bloom, festal?*
> *A vain jest, or holy feast?*
> —*Eugene Warren*

APPENDIX

The Work of Rudolf Laban

Rudolf Laban, the great movement pioneer, has undoubtedly influenced me in writing this book. However, his sixteen movement themes, as ennumerated in his book *Modern Educational Dance* are applicable only to a limited degree to the very young, who lack the mental objectivity and physical know-how to utilize them properly.

Nevertheless *Modern Educational Dance* may be of help to preschool dance teachers. They may be able to use it as a means of discovering interesting varieties of movement which can then be presented in more simple ways to younger children. For example, in this book Rudolf Laban analysed weight-time combinations in detail. The weight of a given movement was said to comprise a fine or a firm touch; the time taken for it was either sudden or sustained. He added a third component pertaining to space and called it direct or indirect (flexible) movement.

With these combinations, countless varieties of movement could be made. Laban used action words to denote them. For example a *flick* would consist of a sudden, flexible movement with a fine touch; a *thrust* would consist of a direct, sudden movement with a firm touch, etc.

He then devised the idea of an Effort Cube, which was representative of the body, and from which all possible *directions* of movement could be made. Thus many permutations of movement description became possible.

Most of those aspects of Rudolf Laban's work which apply to preschoolers have been instinctively included under different guises in these pages.

The following two books are recommended:

Laban, Rudolf. *Modern Educational Dance.* London: Macdonald and Evans, 1963.

Thornton, S. *A Movement Perspective of Rudolf Laban.* London: Macdonald and Evans, 1971.

Bibliography of Books on Childhood Education for general reading interest

Authors of the following books, many of whom are famous pioneers, sometimes disagree with one another in their premises. However, each one has profound perspective of particular facets of learning, and much wisdom.

Jaques-Dalcroze, Emile. *A Rhythm Music and Education.* Great Britain: The Dalcroze Society (Inc.), Paperback Edition, 1973.

Keith Faulkner says in his introduction: "His unique approach to music education undoubtedly stemmed from the fact that he came to teaching as a composer and creative artist. He quickly realized that the musical element of primary appeal to children is rhythm; that the natural response to rhythm is physical, and that the body should be the child's first instrument through which to reflect the movement and nuances in music." This book is an exposition of this idea with method, example, and applications to the arts and education in general.

Montessori, Maria. *Education and Peace.* Chicago: Henry Regnery Company, 1972.

This book deals with early education in the context of world peace and humanity in general, and is based on Maria Montessori's premise—"Establishing a lasting peace is the work of education; all politics can do is keep us out of war."

Montessori, Maria. *The Secret of Childhood.* Indiana: Fides Publishers, Inc., 1966.

This book contains many of Maria Montessori's discoveries in methods of education and particularly emphasizes the potentialities and needs in the young child that seem to have gone unrecognized, and which she strove so hard to develop and fulfil.

Piaget, Jean. *Six Psychological Studies.* New York: Vintage Books/ A Division of Random House, 1968.

In the words of David Elkind in the introduction—"He (Piaget) is not fundamentally a child psychologist concerned with practical issues of child growth and development. He is rather . . . concerned with the nature of knowledge and with the structure and processes by which it is acquired." These essays are rather intricately written, but they are so fascinating that one feels as if one is sifting nuggets of pure gold.

Richmond, P. G. *An Introduction to Piaget.* New York: Basic Books, Inc., 1970.
This book summarises many of Piaget's findings, and is much easier reading than Piaget's original writings.

Suzuki, Shinichi. *Nurtured By Love.* New York: Exposition Press, 1969.
This inspiring book is best described by the words on the cover: "In this trailblazing book, world renowned violinist and teacher Shinichi Suzuki presents the philosophy and principles of his teaching methods for developing the natural abilities of every child.... Professor Suzuki presents convincing evidence to substantiate his view ... that every child is born with ability."

The following four books give background on dance:

Haselbach, Barbara. *Dance Education.* London: Schott and Co. Ltd., 1971.
This book gives basic principles and models for Nursery and Primary School, in the dance field. It provides background information on various types of dance movement and training, discusses different methods, and gives some useful observations and teaching material. It does not deal, however, with the psychology of the very young child, nor offer suitable teaching material at that level.

Boorman, Joyce. *Dance and Language Experience with Children.* Ontario: Longman Canada Ltd., 1973.
Myer Horowitz has this to say in the Preface—"Joyce Boorman has succeeded in writing a truly delightful book about her experiences working with children in the areas of creative dance and language. In addition, her book is an important statement of the nature of learning and teaching." Although the children in Joyce Boorman's classes are in the primary grades, much can be learned from her methods.

Boorman, Joyce. *Dance in the First Three Grades.* Ontario: Longman Canada, Ltd.,1969.

Boorman, Joyce. *Creative Dance in Grades Four to Six* Ontario: Longman Canada, Ltd., 1971.

The above two books deal with creative dance for older children and the basic content of them stems from the work of Rudolf Laban. They are practical and imaginative and are valuable background reading as they show how creative dance can be developed beyond the preschool years.

Recommended Recorded Music, Piano Books, Song Books, and Poetry Books

In preparing the list of suggested Music, Poetry, and Song Books to accompany the dance, it is realized that not all the pieces in any given selection will prove suitable. However, a good proportion of the material suggested is useable. Also what works for one teacher may not work for another, so individual selection must be left to your discretion according to your preference and the class's needs and abilities.

Recorded Music

The following famous selections which were not primarily created for children's dancing, nevertheless contain some useful pieces. Because they are more sophisticated it's helpful if, on percussion, you can beat out the basic rhythms over the sound of the recording.

Rossini arranged by Respighi—*La Boutique Fantasque*

Saint-Saens, Camille—*The Carnival of Animals*

Tchaikovsky, Peter Ilyitch—*The Nutcracker Suite*

The following three piano selections contain some good "mood" background music (for scarf trailing, leaf blowing, snow falling, resting, and listening, etc.)

Debussy, Claude—*Children's Corner*

Schumann, Robert—*Scenes from Childhood*

Grieg, Edvard—*Lyric Suite*

Many Folk Dance albums make excellent dancing music for little ones, because the tunes have simple repetitive rhythms and attractive melodies. One such example is the *South American Flute* record series, put out by Voyage.

Piano Books

Bartok, Bela. *Mikrokosmos* (6 Books). London, New York, Paris: Boosey and Hawkes.
Bartok, Bela. *For Children.* London, New York, Paris: Boosey and Hawkes. Book I—Based on Hungarian Folk Tunes. Book II—Based on Slovakian Folk Tunes.
Prokofiev, Serge. *Music for Children, Opus 65.* New York: Boosey and Hawkes.
Music of our Time (8 Books). Jean Coulthard, David Duke, Joan Hansen. Ontario: Waterloo Music Co. Ltd., 1977–78.
Music for Millions. (Pieces by famous composers in their original form.)
Volume 17—Easy Classics to Moderns. Volume 27—More Easy Classics to Moderns. Volume 37—Classics to Moderns.

Song Books

The Children's Song Book. London, Sidney, Toronto: The Bodley Head, 1961 (Reprinted 1979).
The Golden Song Book. New York: Golden Press, Western Publishing Co. Ltd. (Latest reprinting 1981).

Poetry Books

Come Follow Me—Poems for the Young. London: Bell and Hyman (New Edition February 1984.)
Time for Poetry—A Teacher's Anthology. Chicago: Scott, Foresman and Co. (Third Edition 1968).

Additional copies of this book may be
obtained from the Publisher for

$16.95

plus $2.00 per copy for shipping
and handling

Information regarding bulk order
rates available on request

Please order from:

(In Canada)
Order Department
Windborne Publications
P.O. Box 359,
Heriot Bay, B.C.
V0P 1H0